Your Food
-
My Adventure

PHILIP E. BRADSHAW

Your Food - My Adventure

One Farmer's Journey to Feed the World

Archway Publishing books may be ordered through booksellers or by contacting:

Archway Publishing
1663 Liberty Drive
Bloomington, IN 47403
www.archwaypublishing.com
1 (888) 242-5904

Image 9: Lynn T. Spence / St Louis Post-Dispatch / Polaris

ISBN: 978-1-4808-7951-5 (sc)
ISBN: 978-1-4808-7950-8 (hc)
ISBN: 978-1-4808-7952-2 (e)

Library of Congress Control Number: 2019910509

Print information available on the last page.

Archway Publishing rev. date: 8/23/2019

Dedicated to my family for their love and support and especially to my wife, Linda, for making this journey through life memorable, worthwhile, and fun.

Contents

Foreword ix
Preface xiii
Acknowledgments xv

1 The Trip of a Lifetime 1
2 Mexico Trip Leaves Lasting Impression 7
3 Meeting My Wife, Linda 19
4 Political Rally with Paul Findley 23
5 Starting My Career in Farming 31
6 Marrying Linda and Joining the Army 41
7 Tragedy Helps Refocus My Life 53
8 Strength in Numbers 59
9 Devastating Disease Leads to Leadership Opportunities 71
10 Foot-and-Mouth Disease Eradication Efforts 81
11 The Summit of the Americas 93
12 Trip to Romania 101
13 Checkoff Programs Benefit Farmers and Consumers 111
14 The Soybean Checkoff 119
15 The Soybean Soap Opera 131
16 Trips to Russia and China 141
17 Working to Save the Local Bank 153
18 Interstate Highway and New Philadelphia 159
19 A Walk from Kentucky 169
20 My Journey to Feed the World 181

Foreword

Phil Bradshaw, that "little ol' farm boy" from Pike County (population fifteen thousand), has taken time to tell the story of his remarkable life journey and in so doing celebrates not only his work, but a community of unsung heroes who over the past century emerged from rural America to create a modern food and agricultural system that played a major role in banishing hunger from the lives of countless millions. His tools were simple. He had a clear, pragmatic worldview formed through the daily challenges of life on the farm and a commitment to service drawn from observation of family and community members in a world where service to the greater good was just an expectation of all. He was passionate, visionary, and persistent and made the world a better place.

My association with Phil began in the early 1980s in the ramp-up to the University of Illinois's effort to import unique breeding swine from China for use in our research program. As my career transitioned over time from faculty member in agriculture to senior administrative positions, he was always supportive and a reliable source of wise and absolutely frank advice. Through this association, I came to consider him a friend and respect him as a transformational agricultural leader.

When he began his farming career, food production was largely local or regional in nature, and farming was as much a lifestyle as a profession. He has been a part of the transformation from that midtwentieth century model to the globally integrated food system of today that is capable of feeding the world's population adequately, sustainably, and safely.

He is a lifelong learner who grew from humble origins and relatively modest educational beginnings to a position of national and international policy leadership in at least three domains: animal health, the development of the global soybean production distribution system, and the creation of an international program to provide nutritious soybean protein to the protein-deficient populations of the world. Along the way, he influenced the path of a section of the interstate highway system, participated in opening the doors of the vast Chinese market to US agricultural products, and facilitated the archeological work critical to the establishment of New Philadelphia as a historically significant African-American site. And he contributed to the site being listed as a National Historic Place; a National Historic Landmark, included as a member of the National Park Service Underground Railroad Network to Freedom program; and national legislation being passed by the US Congress and signed by President Obama to study the site to be considered as a unit of the National Park Service.

Bradshaw has a knack for working with the movers and shakers in the agricultural community and with local, state, national, and international elected officials who were often persuaded of the wisdom of his views. As a result, he served on countless advisory committees and commissions formed to address significant policy matters. He was always willing to take on major leadership responsibilities in organizations as diverse as the Illinois Pork Producers Association and the president of AMPS (Adams, Morgan, Pike, and Scott Counties Interstate Highway Association). Without exception these were uncompensated volunteer roles where the only personal gain was the satisfaction of knowing that a necessary job had been well done.

While doing all of this, Bradshaw was a full-time farmer who began his career on borrowed money and grew the operation to be one of the most successful enterprises in Pike County. He tended his hogs, planted and harvested his crops, served his local community, and, with his wife, Linda, raised a family. And then he climbed out of bed the next day to fly off to Washington, DC, Moscow, São Paulo, or countless other destinations to meet with world leaders.

What can we learn from the life of Phil Bradshaw? This account suggests that regardless of one's starting point, integrity, vision, and a willingness to learn and to engage fearlessly can lead to a life of significant positive impact. He should be a source of inspiration for all.

Dr. Robert E. Easter, president emeritus University of Illinois and former chancellor of the University of Illinois and dean of the College of Agricultural, Consumer and Environmental Sciences

Preface

The stories and events of one's life are varied and often difficult to express in writing. This is also true of the progression of food production. Agriculture has changed in so many ways, and the food we eat is so varied that it is almost impossible to tell a complete story of how our food is produced.

This book is a collection of stories and events from my life's journey. It was difficult to decide which stories to include. There was not enough room to tell about a day I spent with Vice President Dan Quayle traveling across Illinois, a trip I took down the Mississippi River from St. Louis to New Orleans on a towboat, or a lengthy conversation at the Republican National Convention with George W. Bush and Oliver North.

My life's journey has paralleled the journey of agriculture's production from being labor intensive to utilizing high technology. This book is about the people that have helped me along the way and have inspired me to want to help others and make a positive difference in the world.

We are so dependent on each other that no one can truly say they did anything by themselves. Farming is no different. Many people helped build the tractors, combines, augers, and buildings; mine and make the fertilizer; improve the genetics; and provide all the things necessary to make my life's work as a farmer possible.

I hope that this book makes you think of all the people working to help feed you and your family every day and that you find the stories and information about agriculture and food production interesting and enlightening.

Preface

Acknowledgments

I would like to thank many people for helping to make this crazy idea of writing a book into a reality.

My good friend Doc Hull for his constant encouragement and proofreading.

Anne Anderson for her help in proofreading and editing.

Tim and LeAnn Maiers of Maiers Ag Consulting for ghostwriting the book.

Rita Frazer for her motivation to take the action needed to start on the book I've always dreamed of writing and for help in finalizing and promoting the book.

Thanks to all the men and women who I have served with on various committees and boards over the years and their dedication to agriculture.

1 The Trip of a Lifetime

Our lives are a series of different journeys that we take; some are short trips, and some are longer. I believe the destination is not as important as what we learn along the way. For this little ol' farm boy from Griggsville, Illinois, located in Pike County in the west central part of the state, a trip to Mexico would not just be the trip of a lifetime but would also have a huge impact on the rest of my life.

It was 1959, and I was headed to Mexico City with my friend Johnny Warton in his green MG TF two-seater sports car. It was August, not long before I was to start back at Western Illinois University (WIU). Johnny and I had taken some great road trips together—to Nashville and Kansas—but this was the biggest road trip for either of us. It included a trek of more than one thousand miles into and out of a foreign country.

The idea to go to Mexico was planted in my mind by our neighbors Wendell and Lola Orr. It's funny how certain people can have an impact on you, even if you don't think they do at the time. Wendell and Lola lived across the gravel road from my family's farm. We didn't socialize much with the Orrs.

Wendell had married into some money, and he and Lola did a lot of traveling. They would come home from their trips to Mexico and tell me and my two brothers about their adventures. This sparked my imagination and instilled a desire to travel to faraway places and have adventures of my own someday.

After Johnny and I dreamed up this crazy idea of driving his car to

Mexico, I talked to the Orrs about it, and they encouraged us to go. They even helped us plan our trip and offered suggestions on where to stay and things to see. My parents weren't really excited about me going. It was a crazy-fool thing to do, but I was twenty years old, and they couldn't really stop me. There were guys uptown who were betting if we would make it back alive. I'm not sure what kind of odds they gave us, but I'm sure it wasn't good.

One thing was for sure: we were not going to travel to Mexico in record time. The little MG had a top speed of about forty-five to fifty miles per hour with normal driving speed around thirty-five to forty miles per hour. Slow and steady was our pace, much like the tortoise in the race with the hare. We could drive about 450 miles a day, barring any major delays. Little did we know the delays would occur once we reached the Mexican border.

It took Johnny and me two and a half days to reach the border town of McAllen, Texas. Upon arrival, we had to purchase insurance for the car and ourselves before we could enter Mexico.

Since I was not over the age of twenty-one, and the car was titled in Johnny's dad's name, the border officials would not sell us the required insurance. We had to go to the post office and have our parents telegraph the proper papers so we could get the insurance. When it was all said and done, it took three days before we could cross the border. That was longer than the time it had taken us to drive from Griggsville to the border.

Traveling into Mexico was very simple at that time. You showed officials a copy of a birth certificate, the title to the car, and proof of insurance. I do not remember them stamping anything or giving us any papers.

Crossing the border had been a major hurdle in this journey, but now we were ready to experience this foreign country we had heard so much about.

We crossed into Mexico at about eight o'clock in the morning with plans to drive to Monterrey that day. The MG had a canvas top and only sat about thirty-six inches off the ground, so everyone on the road could see in our car. We must have been quite a sight—two American boys driving a little green sports car with a steel trunk strapped to the back. There was no doubt we were not from around there.

I forgot to mention the engineering feat of the steel trunk. Since the MG didn't have a trunk or anywhere else to carry a suitcase or supplies, my dad came up with the idea of making a steel trunk and mounting it on the luggage rack on the back. Before we left, we went to the local welding shop, run by a mighty fine man named Robert Wilkins. Mr. Wilkins was a good welder and very creative. He kept busy doing repair work for farmers around the community.

The challenge was that the trunk had to be light enough for the little car to carry but strong enough so that people could not break into it. Mr. Wilkins quickly devised a plan. Then he found some metal that was an eighth-inch thick and very strong and welded up a box about eighteen inches wide by eighteen inches deep and three feet long. He then made a lid for the top that folded around the box so it would not leak and put not one but two padlocks on the box. He then clamped the box to the carrier rack on the back of the little MG.

This project had become a topic of discussion among several men in the community. Mr. Wilkins's shop looked like the NASA scientists working together to try to bring the astronauts home from the Apollo 11 mission. The consensus was that the box was not going to be strong enough to keep someone from stealing it. For an added safety measure, Mr. Wilkins put a chain up to the box and down around the axle of the car and then bolted the chain to the frame under the box. Harry Houdini wouldn't even be able to get the box off the car. Inside the box were clips so we could lift the box off the car and carry it inside the hotel.

Johnny and I had driven about fifty miles into Mexico when we reached the first checkpoint. We pulled over, and two Mexican police officers (or at least two guys dressed like police officers) approached the car. They asked to see our identification, proof of insurance, and travel itinerary. They looked our car all over from top to bottom as if we were trying to smuggle something into the country.

In 1959, I didn't speak a lick of Spanish. Still don't. The problem was that the police officers could not speak a word of English. Looking back at this trip more than fifty years later, it's no wonder my parents were so worried about two foolish farm boys who didn't know where they were going in a foreign country and were unable to speak the language.

The stop must have taken over an hour, and we were getting a little bit nervous because we did not see a car or anybody else around. Finally, they gave us the international sign to move along, and we were back on the road.

We thought we were in the clear. But after another fifty miles, when we were almost to Monterrey, we got stopped by two police officers in the same manner. We went through the same drill all over again, but this time one of the officers reached down in the car and picked up a set of nice binoculars that we had brought. He took them out of the case and started looking around as if he was on a hunting expedition looking for big game. As he was looking through our binoculars, the other officer started motioning for us to move along. We did not want to leave our new binoculars, so we just sat there.

Believe it or not, the officer who was motioning us to move along started to take his pistol out of his holster. I can't speak for Johnny, but I can tell you I was getting nervous and a little shaky. I reached out to my left, past Johnny, who was in the driver's seat, for my binoculars. The officer growled at me and then stuck his hand out. It took me a second to realize that he wanted money. I grabbed a five-dollar bill, which was a lot of money in those days, and slipped it into his hand. His stern face lightened, and he handed the binoculars to me. Then we were back on the way. I found out later that tipping or giving the officers a little money was standard procedure. In the end, no harm was done. It was money well spent.

After a long day on the road and the stress of navigating the foreign roads and customs, we were both ready for a nice, soft bed at the hotel in Monterrey, where we had reservations. This was a hotel that the Orrs had recommended, so we knew that it would be a nice place, and the staff would speak English. We had a little trouble finding the place and finally arrived well after dark.

We went to the registration desk to check in, and the young man behind the desk spoke English very well. His voice was music to my ears. But what he said was not good. They did not have any vacancies. The three-day delay crossing the border had made us late and had messed up our reservations. What were we going to do?

The young man said he would find us another place to stay and began calling other hotels. After several calls, he gave us the name of a motel on the edge of Monterrey. He tried to give us instructions on how to get there, but we were confused and overwhelmed. He finally left from behind the desk and got in his car. We followed him for quite a way across Monterrey to this old, rundown, dilapidated motel.

The motel was clean, but it was nothing like what we were hoping to have. No one spoke English, so the young man talked to the lady who owned the motel and got us squared away. The lady at the motel was very nice, and everyone treated us very well. She was afraid that someone would damage our little car, so she put it directly next to the office and put her German shepherd dog right beside it to guard it. We stayed in Monterrey two nights.

Our next destination was Mexico City. We planned to drive to San Luis Potosi and spend the night and then drive the rest of the way to Mexico City the next day. There was a lot of traffic on the highway between Monterrey and Mexico City. It was a little nerve-wracking driving our tiny MG among the big old Mexican trucks and old cars, some of which did not have headlights or taillights, but we made it without a problem.

We got to our hotel where the lady at the motel in Monterrey had made reservations for us. We had just gotten the keys to our room and were starting to unhook our steel trunk from the car when five college-age American girls drove up in a nice, big, fancy new Pontiac car. They had been searching for a room and had already been several places and could find no vacancies. They were scared to death of driving on to Mexico City after dark, so being the nice guys that we were, we offered for them to stay with us. That idea went over like a lead balloon, but it was worth a try!

The hotel clerk spoke some English and called around to see if they could find another room. There were no vacancies because there was a big golf tournament in town, which we come to find out, is why these girls were here. Johnny and I thought it was funny that they did not have a hotel reservation before they came. Finally, Johnny and I said they could have our room, and we would drive on to Mexico City, where we had a reservation for the next night.

We called the hotel in Mexico City and confirmed that we could arrive one night early. While we were doing this, the lady from the motel we stayed at in Monterrey called the hotel to check if we had arrived in one piece. It amazed us that this lady thought enough of us to call and check in on us and make sure we were all right. The hotel clerk told her what we had done—gave up our room for these girls who didn't have a room, and were going to drive to Mexico City.

Johnny and I put our trunk back on the little MG and started out in the dark night driving to Mexico City. It made us kind of nervous to be on a strange road, in a strange country, not sure exactly where we were going. By this time, though, we had realized that the people in Mexico were very nice and helpful, and this helped calm our fears. We would be even further surprised by the hospitality of the Mexican people when we arrived in Mexico City.

Mexico Trip Leaves Lasting Impression

It's funny what you remember about your childhood. I can't tell you what grades I got on my report cards or how many points I scored in a basketball game. Most of my memories from my childhood involve my family and growing up on our farm in Pike County.

I can specifically remember when my grandfather got two Massey Harris 22 tractors and put cultivators on both of them. My brothers and I were getting old enough to start cultivating corn, and grandpa wanted to make sure that he didn't miss the chance to put us to work.

I can also remember back in 1947 the last time that we threshed wheat before we got a combine. I watched the guys hauling the shock bundles of wheat from the fields to the threshing machine. It was an impressive operation. The threshing machine left large circular straw piles beside where the machine sat to thresh the grain. The next spring my mom and brothers and I would plant cucumbers all around those straw piles, and we'd pick cucumbers all summer to make pickles.

Like most other farmers in the Midwest in the 1940s and 1950s, our family raised quite a bit of livestock—mostly cows, chickens, and pigs. The livestock helped diversify the farm and provide another source of income. Although as a boy, I thought livestock was just something for me and my brothers to do to keep us out of trouble. My dad lived by the principle "idle hands are the devil's workshop," so we rarely had a time that we weren't busy. I don't ever remember telling my parents that I was bored. If I would have uttered those words, there would have been a pile of work for me to do somewhere on that farm.

My dad and his brother, my uncle Walter, raised one thousand to twelve hundred pigs per year, which was a lot of hogs for the times. They raised them on the twenty acres that my dad had purchased along with our house when we moved out to the countryside in 1942.

Pork Production—Then and Now

The majority of farms in the Midwest during the 1940s, '50s and '60s raised pigs. They were a good fit for Illinois farmers because pigs could consume the crops grown on farms and did not require a lot of capital investment. At that time all the pigs were raised outside in dirt lots.

The majority of pigs raised in the 1950s and 1960s were housed outside in huts like these called "Pike County huts." The name came from the large number of huts being used in Pike County. (Photo courtesy of Larry Borrowman.)

Water and feed had to be hauled to them daily. Sometimes the pigs would be raised in the timber with a creek or stream for a watering source. There was no way to contain the manure. When it rained, the manure would wash away in the rainwater. There was very little vegetation in the pig lots because the pigs would root in the dirt and dig mudholes to keep cool in the summer. This caused a lot of erosion. This type of pork production was very damaging to the environment.

The demand for more food worldwide really started increasing after President Nixon devalued the dollar in 1971. Corn, soybean, and wheat acres began increasing, and demand for pork increased. Farmers answered this challenge by increasing our number of pigs produced. This meant increasing the number of pigs raised on an acre, which in turn caused even more damage to vegetation in the fields and led to more manure running off into streams. This, in addition to more land being put into crops, was decreasing wildlife habitat, which was concerning to farmers and the rest of society. Coyotes and other predators were eating pigs at a high rate in outside lots and pastures. These problems along with the cost of hauling or piping water to the pigs, keeping the manure out of the streams, and the high mortality and sickness rate from pigs being exposed to extreme weather caused me and many other farmers to start raising our pigs inside buildings.

We built our first hog barn in 1974. It was a partially slatted barn, which meant that one-third of the floor had concrete slats that allowed the manure to go through three-quarter-inch gaps in the floor. The rest of the floor was solid concrete. The manure would fall through the slats into the concrete storage pit. It would be stored there until it was vacuumed out and transferred to a wagon. The wagon would haul the manure to the crop fields to be applied as fertilizer. This was much better for the environment and prevented the manure from going into the streams. We could now control the manure and use it, as farmers have for thousands of years, as a natural fertilizer.

Today's modern hog barns have further improved how we care for the pigs and environment with the use of technology.

Today the majority of pigs are housed inside climate-controlled barns like these that keep pigs comfortable and healthy. (Photo courtesy of Tim Maiers.)

Fans and misters keep the pigs comfortable in the summertime, and heaters keep the pigs warm in the winter. Sensors constantly monitor the temperature in the barns and can be monitored and changed on a farmer's smart phone. The manure is applied using Global Positioning System (GPS), which can vary the amount of manure applied according to the soil type and amount of nutrients in the soil. Farmers use computer-generated manure management plans, which fine-tune the nutrients in the manure with the nutrient needs of the growing crops.

This progress in pork production has benefitted the consumer with healthy, nutritious, and affordable pork products.

It was a lot of work to get a pig ready to sell, so it was a big deal when the day came to load up the pigs and haul them to market. We usually hauled our pigs to the stockyards in East St. Louis. Most farmers would haul their pigs in their own trucks or ride along with the trucker to watch their livestock be sold. Farmers would stay overnight to see their hogs sell the next morning to a packer for processing. It also gave the farmers an opportunity to do a little partying in the big city.

As a nine-year-old I can remember riding along to East St. Louis with my uncle Walter in Grandpa's two-ton 1948 Dodge truck. It had a sixteen-foot bed and hauled approximately thirty-five pigs weighing 225 to 230 pounds each. My cousin Sam would often ride along. His dad drove, and we would sit on a piece of railroad tie placed on the seat so we could see out the windows of the old truck.

The trip to East St. Louis from Griggsville was an interesting 110-mile journey along the highway that ran beside the Illinois River most of the way. The route took us through Alton, Illinois, and there was a big hill in town that the trucks had to climb to reach the final destination of the stockyards in East St. Louis. The old trucks with their full loads of market-ready pigs would have to shift clear down to granny gear, the lowest gear, to make it up the hill. I could have run faster than that old truck lumbering up that hill. There were many times when I questioned if we would make it and worried about rolling backward and seeing the pigs rolling down the hill.

This was a well-traveled route for many farmers from Illinois that were hauling pigs to East St. Louis. Every one of us followed that same ol' route, and the locals knew it. The slow-moving trucks filled with tasty pork chops and bacon were too enticing for some. It became a common occurrence for thieves to climb on the trucks and throw a 225-pound pig over the back, providing tasty pork for their families for many months.

In the Old West the term "riding shotgun" was coined to describe the person sitting next to the driver of the stagecoach to protect the passengers and to keep the precious cargo from being stolen. As the hog trucks approached Alton, oftentimes someone would get out and "ride shotgun" in the back of the truck to dissuade anyone from stealing one of the precious pigs.

My uncle Walter told a story about a man riding in the back of the truck carrying a baseball bat. When the thief put his fingers over the side of the truck racks to pull himself up, the man hit the thief's fingers with the bat. It only took a few swings and that took care of the problem.

I thought of those pigs being escorted to market as Johnny and I drove up an incline entering Mexico City in the dark. We would have given anything for an escort to our final destination—a supposedly nice hotel somewhere in Mexico City. As we neared the city, we noticed that two police cars began to follow us. My first thought was here we go again with the so-called inspection. Both police cars pulled alongside of us. I cringed and tensed up as I braced for what was next, but the most amazing thing happened.

Both officers smiled and waved and motioned for us to follow them. The first car pulled in front of us and the second car pulled directly behind us, both with blue lights flashing. We were quickly in the middle of a police escort!

We were pretty sure that they didn't have us confused for someone else since our little green MG was the only one of its kind on the Mexican highways. I had never had a police escort before, and it was quite the experience. We drove straight to the hotel arriving about eleven thirty or midnight. We got out and gave each police officer five dollars, which in those days was probably two days' wages, but we were pleased to have the help and elated that we had made it to our destination safely.

Johnny and I determined that the lady that owned the motel in Monterrey must have been very influential. Fate had taken us to her motel, and she was looking after us like our own mothers, even arranging a police escort to repay us for our kindness in giving up our room for the group of girls. Who says that nice deeds go unnoticed!

The accommodations were a five-star hotel that Mr. Orr had recommended to us and were very nice. He had not led us astray. This was the first time on our trip that we were able to stay in a hotel that he had recommended.

We had lined up a couple tours of the city that departed from the hotel. This was really the first extensive sightseeing that we had done on our trip. We got to see most of Mexico City, and we only had two minor incidents while there, which for us wasn't too bad.

The first incident was at the National Autonomous University of Mexico. Johnny stepped off the city bus that we were traveling on with our translator and tour guide. Either I was moving too slowly or the bus started moving too fast, but as I stepped off of the bus, it started to move and threw me into a big round marble pillar. I fell hard to the ground and got a big goose egg on my forehead. The tour guide was very nervous and concerned about my condition. She took me to the university hospital, where they looked at me and decided I did not have a concussion and would be all right.

The second incident involved an airplane. Johnny and I had decided to fly to Acapulco on the West Coast. We got to the airport with no problems. As we boarded the plane we noticed mud and dirt on the outside of the plane. We thought that was unusual since the plane was sitting on a concrete runway. We never did find out why it was so muddy. Once inside the plane we were greeted with about twenty people on board who seemed to have brought everything they owned with them, including live chickens! As the plane started taxiing down the runway, I thought to myself, *How will this little plane be able to get in the air with all these people, luggage, and livestock?*

I remember how noisy it was, and suddenly the plane started to shake and shimmy violently. The pilot tried to stop the plane as quickly as he could. Come to find out, the plane had blown a tire. We were lucky that it had happened on takeoff rather than landing. Johnny and I got back to the terminal, decided the hell with it, grabbed a taxi back to our hotel, and never did go to Acapulco.

Mexico was a very impoverished country, much like it is today. The sanitary conditions were very poor, and we were afraid to drink the water. In 1959 you had to get certain shots to travel to Mexico, and I think if you didn't get those shots you could not come back into the United States. Johnny and I went to the doctor at WIU before we left. This doctor was semiretired from the military and had been a medical doctor in the army for almost thirty years, serving in World War II and the Korean War.

He gave us some good advice for staying healthy in a foreign country. His advice was "never take a bite of food outside the United States unless you wash it down with some good old strong alcohol." I have followed this advice all my life. Now I do not know if this helped or not, but in all my worldly travels I have only gotten sick from food poisoning once.

The trade between the United States and Mexico has greatly increased from 1959 until now. It makes sense that our neighboring country would be one of our biggest trading partners. The leaders of both countries should be commended for agreeing to sign and fully implement the North

American Free Trade Agreement (NAFTA) which took effect on January 1, 1994, and was fully implemented in 2008. Under NAFTA, Mexico and the United States have eliminated all trade restricting tariffs and quantitative restrictions on agricultural goods. NAFTA is one of the most successful free-trade agreements in history and has contributed to significant increases in agricultural trade and investment between the United States, Canada, and Mexico. It has benefited farmers, ranchers, and consumers throughout North America. I believe that this increase in trade will continue into the future and raise incomes in all of North America.

I also believe that if agricultural trade between Canada, Mexico, and the United States would end, it would be devastating to the economy of all three countries.

Importance of US and Mexico ag trade

Mexico is the United States' third-largest agricultural export market. US sales of food and farm products to Mexico totaled a record $19 billion in fiscal year 2017. Top products included corn, soybeans, pork, dairy, and beef.

US imports of agricultural products from Mexico totaled $25 billion in 2017, our largest supplier of agricultural imports. Leading categories include: other fresh fruit ($6 billion), fresh vegetables ($5.5 billion), wine and beer ($3.3 billion), snack foods ($2.1 billion), and processed fruit and vegetables ($1.5 billion).[1]

NAFTA has and can continue to benefit both Mexico and the United States with increased exports to the benefit of both countries. Consumers benefit with better year-round product choices at better prices.

More than 64 percent of the fruits and vegetables imported from Mexico are during the December to May winter months, providing products that are not available in the United States.

The majority of agricultural imports from Mexico to the United States do not compete with American industries for three main reasons:

1. They are products of specific American consumer choice that are not available in the United States such as Corona beer.
2. They are products not grown/produced in the United States such as raw chocolate and coffee.
3. They are products available on a seasonal basis, such as wintertime fresh fruits and vegetables.

Overview of US ag exports to Mexico courtesy of USDA FAS

Farming in Mexico was very primitive and was done mostly by hand and horses and donkeys. We saw lots of donkey carts and horse carts on all the roads, even in Mexico City. There were a lot of open-air markets and roadside stands all over Mexico. We saw people who were malnourished everywhere. At this time, there was very little food crossing the border between the United States and Mexico. Consumers in the United States were afraid to purchase much food from Mexico because of the sanitary conditions.

Farmers are notorious for driving through the country and gazing at the crops. This allows them to compare their neighbors' crops to their own. I remember checking out the Mexican corn crop and thinking that it looked terrible. The corn looked so bad that Johnny and I thought we should have filled our little car up with seed corn and showed them how to raise a good ear of corn. However, we did see some good-looking green beans.

Seeing the many hungry people in Mexico left a lasting impression on me. It sparked a desire in me to try to do something about it. I believed that increased trade between our countries would provide more opportunities for the Mexican people to improve their lives and their diets. I didn't realize that several years later, I would have an opportunity to help promote that trade.

In the 1980s I had been meeting and working with Illinois Governor Jim Thompson to get the Central Illinois Expressway (I-72) completed from Champaign, Illinois, to Hannibal, Missouri. More on that later. I had told Governor Thompson about my trip to Mexico in 1959 and how I felt Illinois needed to encourage more companies to do business in Mexico. Lieutenant Governor George Ryan had been asked by Governor Thompson to lead a team to look at the future of rural Illinois. I was asked by the governor to serve on the Future of Rural Illinois task force and attended twenty out of the twenty-two meetings held around the state with the lieutenant governor.

This occurred during the same time Illinois was working on opening a trade office in Mexico City. I remember being in Mexico City with Lieutenant Governor Ryan meeting with a number of Mexican government and business leaders. After the more formal dinner and activities were over, the Mexican folks showed George and me how to drink tequila with lemon. It was an interesting night, and I didn't do very well keeping up in drinking with the locals.

In 1989, Illinois opened one of the first state trade offices in Mexico City. I believe it was the first nonborder state to open an office in Mexico. The trade office has been and still is a big help to companies doing or wanting to do business in Mexico.

I believe this has been one of the most successful international trade offices Illinois has established. In 1998 I had the pleasure of going with Governor Jim Edgar to Mexico on a trade mission to see the trade office at its best. Amparo Garza Lang has been the ag director in the office since it opened. She worked day and night to get more Illinois ag products sold to Mexico.

One evening several years later on my way back from speaking on an animal health program in southern Mexico and traveling alone. I called

Amparo. She took me to dinner and wanted to have a big American grain-fed steak. We had a twenty-two-ounce American steak and a bottle of Mexican beer—a great international combination. We had no salad or potatoes, just steak. She said, "Let the people in this nice big restaurant see us eat this grain-fed steak." I had been on a US Meat Export Federation (USMEF) trip to Mexico with US chefs and University of Illinois meat professors to help train hotels and restaurants how to prepare US meat cuts years before. Of all the organizations I have had some involvement with; I think USMEF is one of the best for the US farmers. I'll provide more details on that later in the book.

Trade wasn't a top priority on my mind while Johnny and I visited the University of Mexico and toured Mexico City. Touring the city had been my favorite part of the entire trip. After seven days of adventure in Mexico, it was time to head back home. I had thoroughly enjoyed the time away, but I missed my family and friends and definitely missed my mom's home cooking.

When we got ready to leave Mexico City, our little MG would not start. We thought it was a bad connection on the battery but had no luck fixing it. We had a mechanic look at it. He wiggled the battery wire, and it started right off. We felt kind of stupid but were glad that the car was running again.

We started for home ready for the long journey back to Pike County hoping for a smooth return trip. That lasted until the first time we stopped to fill up for gas. Johnny went to start the MG, and it would not start. We wiggled the battery wires just like the mechanic had done and tried everything we could think of to get it running, but nothing worked.

The last resort was to try to push it to get it started. Johnny sat in the driver's seat with the clutch shoved in and the car in gear. I started pushing the little car with all my might. Once it got rolling at a decent speed, Johnny popped the clutch, and it sputtered to life.

We took turns pushing that dang car to get it started all the way back to Griggsville. We drove from Mexico City to Monterrey and then on to northern Texas and then north to Illinois. Johnny seemed to be having a hard time seeing, so I did most of the driving. The journey home took us about three and a half days with the little car averaging forty miles per hour. By the way, we felt even more stupid when Mr. Wilkins looked at the little car after we got home. He told us that all we had to do was just tighten the screw a little on the battery, and it would start fine, which it did up until Johnny sold the car.

Being back home made me realize what a significant impact this trip had on my life. I definitely appreciated my family and my country more than I did when I left. I got home just in time to help with baling the third cutting of alfalfa hay. Baling hay was usually a hot, dirty job that I dreaded, but this time it didn't seem to bother me as much.

In early September, I got ready to go back to college for my junior year. Johnny decided not to go back to school that fall because he was still having trouble with his vision. He wasn't very sick at that time, but he got worse as the winter went on. Come to find out Johnny had a brain tumor that was causing his vision trouble. Sadly, Johnny passed away three days after brain surgery in the spring of 1960, not even one year after our trip. I'm forever grateful that we had the many adventures that we did, and those memories of our time together are something I've always cherished.

This is the actual MG TF car that Phil and Johnny drove on their one-thousand-mile plus adventure from Griggsville, Illinois, to Mexico. (Photo courtesy of Phil Bradshaw.)

Meeting My Wife, Linda

I ranked sixth in my 1957 high school graduating class, sixth out of twenty-five students. This was not great, but it could have been worse; that pretty well sums up my studies in high school. However, my grades were good enough to get me a four-year tuition scholarship to WIU.

WIU is located in Macomb, Illinois, which is only seventy miles north of Griggsville. The location made it a popular university for many graduating seniors in the west-central part of the state. I majored in agriculture education, and initially I wanted to be a high school ag teacher. I also decided to double major in business administration. I thought a business degree could always be useful in the real world. Throughout college, I took as many business classes as I did agriculture classes.

WIU did not offer a vocational agriculture degree, because at that time it did not have the facilities needed for the vocational training. Many of the agriculture students transferred to the University of Illinois or Southern Illinois University at the end of their sophomore year, so they could get vocational agriculture training, which included training in shop classes such as welding and carpentry. WIU had a good education program, but I did not have the accreditation to be a vocational agriculture teacher, just the qualifications to be an agriculture teacher. Since I didn't have a vocational ag teacher degree, I couldn't have been an FFA adviser. I stayed at WIU all four years because it was a lot cheaper than transferring to the University of Illinois, and I did not want to accumulate a lot of debt before I graduated.

I worked hard to pay my own living expenses through college and did all that I could to save a buck here and there. I lived in apartments all but one summer term. Six of us lived together the first two years. We did our own cooking, cleaning, laundry, and other household duties. This kept the cost down, and since most of us went home every weekend and brought back food from home, or we went hunting and shot squirrels or rabbits, dressed them, and brought them back to the apartment to eat that week, my food bill wasn't much either.

My older brother, Fred, had gone to the army and also had gone to a technical school in Quincy, Illinois, before he started at WIU a year after I did. To make money while at college, Fred and I cut down hedge trees off of the land that is now near the WIU Student Union. We cut the trees into fence posts and sold them to local farmers.

While home on weekends, holidays, and any college breaks, Fred and I cut pulpwood from trees along the creek on our farm. The pulpwood came from soft trees such as willows, cottonwoods, and sycamores. Grandpa and Dad furnished the truck, chainsaw, and tractor to help us. After cutting the trees, we would haul the wood twenty-five miles away to Pearl, Illinois, where they had a big pulpwood chopper. After the pulpwood went through the chopper, it was loaded onto railroad cars and then taken to mills to be made into paper. This was a major part of our income while we were in college.

I was not a very good student the first two years of college. My inability to spell and my poor grammar and reading ability slowed me down. I still think this was from poor teachers in the lower grades where I did not learn phonics. Unbeknownst to me, that trip to Mexico was going to help me become a much better student for the rest of my life.

Going back to college after the Mexico trip caused me mixed emotions. On one hand, I was ready to return to a sense of normalcy and routine. On the other hand, I felt ready to take on the world and was ready for something much bigger. The trip had instilled a newfound confidence in me. I believed if I could make it for a week in Mexico that I could not just survive but wholeheartedly succeed at college and beyond.

Like most other students at WIU, I would go home for the weekends. This gave me lots of opportunities to share stories from the trip to Mexico with family, neighbors, and friends. My trip with Johnny had become well-known throughout a great deal of Pike County. News of our adventures had spread even without the use of today's viral videos or social media networks. Back in those days we had to rely on the best form of spreading information—by word of mouth, gossiping and hearsay!

There was a group sponsored by the University of Illinois Extension Service for young adults called Rural Youth. They asked me to speak about our trip to Mexico at one of their meetings in the Pike County Farm Bureau building. I think they were hard pressed to find a speaker, but I always loved a chance to reminiscence about the trip. There were forty or fifty people in attendance at the meeting. Most of the people there were my age—early twenties.

One young lady seemed to take a special interest in my trip, and I thought she was also a little interested in me. I remember that she was sitting near the front of the room and was very attentive. After the meeting, she came up to me and introduced herself as Linda Bradburn and asked me lots of questions about the trip. We started talking, and I asked her if she would like me to take her home. I did, and then I offered to take her back to school in Quincy the next night, and just like that we were dating.

Linda later told me that she had always wanted to travel the world, and after listening to my presentation, she thought I was going to go places. She was right. Over our fifty-eight years of marriage we have traveled to Europe several times, to most countries in South America, and to Australia. We have traveled to all fifty states. We went to Hawaii several times while I was consulting with a company out of New Zealand that wanted to raise hogs on the island of Molokai.

Linda went to Pittsfield High School and graduated from Gem City Business College in Quincy. After graduating she got a job at Moorman Manufacturing. Neither one of us had a car of our own, so each of us had to share the family car. Her folks would take her back and forth to work in Quincy, or she would ride with someone else. My brother, Fred, had a new Chevrolet Bel Air four-door with two sun visors and push-button radio that he used to take a carload back and forth to college every weekend. There was always a full car. We all gave Fred a little money to ride, but I may not have been as reliable of a funder as I should have been.

About all Linda and I did while we were dating was going back and forth to Quincy for the two years before we married. To say that I was frugal was an understatement. I was so tight with my money that I stopped chewing gum because it cost too much. Linda's family had very little money, so she was more frugal than I was. I never smoked or drank alcohol because I could not afford it.

In the fall of 1960, I was starting my student teaching in Bushnell, Illinois, and needed a car. I purchased a new Chevrolet Biscayne for $1,700. I am proud to say I paid cash. It was a nice car, but it was the cheapest new one that I could find. The car had two luxury items—automatic transmission and AM radio with no push buttons. It only had one sun visor, but thankfully it did have two doors!

Dating Linda was one of the best and biggest changes in my life. Not only had my social life improved greatly but so did my grades. She helped me with my spelling and grammar. After we started dating I went from a low average student to almost a straight A student. After all these years she is still my best friend and keeps me from showing how bad of a speller and grammar person I is. (I mean I am. She caught that when she proofread the book.)

4

Political Rally with Paul Findley

It's been said that the world is run by those who show up. People who are willing to get involved, be present, attend a meeting, and make their voices heard have helped shape this great nation. Think of the millions and millions of people who have volunteered their time to serve their country, their church, their school, or a local organization and the positive impacts that this has had on so many people.

For me, attending one political rally for a little-known congressional candidate allowed me numerous chances to get involved and to try to make a positive difference. Through these efforts, I hope in some small way I have helped make the world a better place.

I didn't realize at the time how this one rally would set the stage for so many things in my life. It provided me experiences that I never could have imagined were possible, including meeting many presidents and traveling around the world.

While at WIU in the fall of 1959, I saw a flyer posted in the student union, Sherman Hall, that caught my attention. The flyer announced that Paul Findley was running for Congress and was going to hold a political rally later in the week in the auditorium of Sherman Hall. While I did not know Paul personally, I knew of him and had seen him once before. He was the editor of the Pike County newspaper and was active in my local community. He had been involved in the Rotary Club when I was in high school. I once heard Paul give a speech about Abraham Lincoln, and it sparked a desire in me to be in politics.

Paul had previously run for the state senate and lost but now in 1960 was running for US Congress. I decided to attend the rally to show my support for this hometown guy. It's not every day that someone you know is running for Congress.

The rally was during the middle of the day, which was an odd time to have a rally, if you ask me. I wandered over to the auditorium, getting there early so that I would get a good seat. Upon arriving I was surprised to see very few people there. I saw the red, white, and blue bunting and "Findley for Congress" signs, so I knew that I was in the right place.

There ended up being only four people in total that attended the rally—myself; Paul Findley; Don Marshall, who was the chairman of the Department of Political Science at WIU; and Don Norton, who went on to get his PhD in political science and served as Paul's chief of staff and helped run his campaigns. This was a far cry from the major political rally that I had envisioned, but even though it was a small rally, it had a large impact on me. This was a good lesson that sometimes it's not the number of people that attend an event that makes it successful.

After meeting Paul and hearing about his political views and witnessing his enthusiasm for what he was doing, I pledged my full support of his candidacy. I became involved in his campaign and helped organize the Farmers for Findley group. I talked to farmers about Paul and urged them to support him.

After that rally I became involved with the college Republican Club at WIU. One of the programs Paul was promoting as part of his political platform was a way to dispose of the grain the US government was holding in storage. The United States Department of Agriculture (USDA) had purchased and stored a large volume of grain, mostly corn and wheat, to help keep grain prices high, but it also kept grain prices from getting even higher. When the price of corn reached a certain level, the USDA would sell the corn it had in storage, and then the price of corn would go back down. This program was a way for the government to control the price of commodities and to some degree that meant the price of food. Paul and I agreed that the United States needed to change our farm policy so the government did not control the price of grain or food.

Later in the fall of 1960, I attended a meeting at Chicago Loyola

University to hear Senator Barry Goldwater speak about the future of the Republican Party and the country. A fairly large group of mostly college-age students was in attendance. Senator Goldwater was late arriving, so someone asked me to explain Congressman-elect Paul Findley's farm policy proposal. I was not well prepared for this impromptu speech, but I had presented a similar speech to a small group earlier in the day. I gave what I think was a good description of current farm programs and Paul's proposal to get the federal government out of the grain business. I remember feeling good about being a part of the political process of sharing ideas and trying to educate people about a change that I believed needed to be made in our government.

Paul's proposal was to let farmers "purchase" the grain in storage back from the government for not planting all their acreage. The idea was that a farmer could sign up for the program and decide not to plant all of his corn acres. For those acres that were not planted, the USDA would give the farmer the corn he would have produced on the acres that were setting idle to feed his animals or to sell on the open market. Paul's idea did not move forward at that time. It did become a program under the farm program that US Ag Secretary John Block worked on many years later.

Findley not only won the election of the US Congressional Twentieth District in 1960 but went on to serve twenty-two years in Congress. Don Marshall, who had attended that small rally at WIU, went on to serve as Paul's chief of staff for part of that time. Don Norton, also one of the four attendees at the rally, became Paul's chief of staff after Don Marshall left the position. Paul lost his bid for reelection in 1982 by only fourteen hundred votes to Dick Durbin. Durbin went on to serve six terms in Congress before being elected to the US Senate in 1996.

If I had to pick four people that have had the greatest impact on my life, it would have to be my uncle Clyde, Grandpa Sam, Dad, and Paul Findley. Paul has served as my mentor and has been a close friend. I have been fortunate to have had many close interactions with Paul, including trips to Russia and China.

Paul and I are both pretty serious people, usually sticking to the task at hand. We enjoyed working together and have kept in contact over the years. Paul is in his nineties now and has remained active and only recently moved into a nursing home in Jacksonville, Illinois. In 2014 I took him to the University of Missouri to a meeting of the Board for International Food and Agriculture Development (BIFAD). BIFAD advises the US Agency for International Development (USAID) on agriculture and higher education issues pertinent to food insecurity in developing countries. Brady J. Deaton, then chancellor of the University of Missouri at Colombia, was chairman of BIFAD.

When Paul was in Congress, he helped pass legislation forming this group of educational institutions tasked to work together for agricultural development around the world and to help collaboratively find solutions to the world's hunger problem. It was a nice opportunity for Paul to see the collective work of these groups that were spearheaded from the legislation that he initiated. It also gave us time to reminiscence about our many years of working together.

Deep down I've always wanted to be a politician, but I never ran for office. There are a lot of things to not like about politics, but one thing I do admire is that at its basic level politics is about making a positive difference on issues and in people's lives. People often have a bad perception about politics due to the constant negative press. I didn't want to subject myself or my family to the negativity that comes with the territory.

I don't like being involved in win or lose situations, and our political system inherently creates winners and losers. When two candidates run for political office, one candidate will get the most votes and be declared the winner; however, even the candidate who loses has also contributed some ideas or thoughts to the political process and to the debate.

To be successful in the business world, you look to create win-win opportunities, where both parties gain something. That's usually not the case in politics. Watch C-SPAN sometime and listen to the rhetoric that is being spouted by both parties on any given issue. Whether it's health care, immigration reform, trade policy, or one of the many issues facing our country, the Democrats or Republicans have to "win" on an issue so they can use it in their next campaign to win reelection.

In reality nothing gets passed without some type of compromise, but it is often spun by the media as which side came out victorious rather than looking at what is best for the entire country and society as a whole.

This leads to continued bickering and fewer bipartisan efforts and more gridlock on issues.

While I never ran for an elected office, I did throw my hat in the ring several times for an appointed government position. I applied for the Illinois director of agriculture job in earnest three times; however, the timing just never was quite right. The first time, in 1976, Governor Jim Thompson said he would consider me for the position, but John Block, a farmer from Knox County, Illinois, came on the scene. He had graduated from West Point and came back to the home farm and expanded the farming operation rapidly. He got the position of Illinois director of Ag in 1976. In 1980 President Reagan appointed Block US secretary of agriculture. I think John was like many farmers who had expanded their farms in the 1960s. Then in the 1970s inflation was at record levels, as high as 10 to 15 percent, and interest rates went from 6 to 8 percent to 18 to 20 percent in the 1980s.

Farmers that did not have sizable equity could not survive 18 to 20 percent interest rates. Land values decreased by nearly 50 percent in some instances. This all happened while John Block was US secretary of agriculture. I truly believe if he would not have been a farmer suffering on his home farm like the rest of us, you would have seen total chaos in rural America in the 1980s. Many families lost the farm that had been in their family for generations. John Block was and is one of the most capable men that I have ever met, and he outshone me in lots of ways.

Once John became a member of President Reagan's cabinet, that created an opening for the Illinois director of ag. I applied again with Governor Thompson's administration and thought I had a pretty good shot, but as often is the case in politics, it's not what you know but who you know. Larry Werries was a farmer from Morgan County and farmed next to the Baise family farm. Gary Baise was a very prominent Republican in Washington, DC, and Gary's brother, Greg, was the chief of staff for Governor Thompson. Greg really wanted Larry to get the director of ag position. I didn't think that Larry had the experiences and qualifications that I did, but since the governor's chief of staff had a candidate that he wanted to get the job, Larry got the position. Larry served as Illinois director of agriculture until the end of the Thompson administration.

When Jim Edgar became governor in 1991, I applied again, thinking the third time would be the charm. I thought this was my chance because I knew Jim Edgar and had been in several meetings with him over the years. But as had been the case before, things didn't quite work out. Becky Doyle had run for state representative and lost. Running a campaign is expensive and she had accumulated some debt. I believe that the Republicans felt they owed her something. She was appointed to the position and did a fine job.

As recently as 2015, there was another opening at the Illinois director of ag position when Philip Nelson resigned. Many people asked me if I was interested in applying, but at that time, at age seventy-six and being involved in several other projects, I didn't need the job and told them I wasn't interested, although I would have liked to prove that I could do the job.

Everyone finds their own passion that motivates them. What motivates me to be involved in the political system? I think I'm still trying to prove that I'm as good as the politicians are. I'm still trying to prove that I have something to contribute.

I have had many people tell me that I have had more influence on agricultural issues than if I had actually been a politician. One time on a trip to Washington, DC, I was sitting around chatting with several prominent ag leaders, including two former US secretaries of agriculture. They told me that I probably have had more of an impact in the long haul on agriculture than they did, because they always had to mess with the bureaucratic government process to get things done. Whereas when I saw a problem or a need, I was able to work directly on a solution by using various resources, including the government and other organizations, to address the issue at hand.

We never know how a chance encounter can lead to a course correction for our life's journey. From the day that I attended the small rally at WIU until today, Paul Findley has been part of my inspiration for getting involved in issues and trying to help be part of the solution and not just complain about the problems.

Phil, Linda, and daughters, Lisa and Cindy, visit with Congressman Paul Findley in DC. (Photo courtesy of Phil Bradshaw.)

5

Starting My Career in Farming

Have you ever stopped to think about all the different food that you eat in a day? Take a second and jot down the food you have consumed in the last twenty-four hours. Now think about where all that food came from and what it took to grow, raise, process, and transport all of it.

Food in the United States and other developed countries has become a given, a right, something that most consumers don't even think about. I believe that most people take for granted that the grocery store shelves will always be full. Think of the chaos that would ensue if your local grocery store had a limited amount of food available to purchase on a weekly basis. Sometimes you hear of customers fighting over the last ham that is on sale before Christmas, but it's not like there aren't other hams available to buy. There's a big difference between fighting over the last ham that is on sale or the last ham in the store.

Food is a good bargain for the American consumer, especially compared to other goods and services that we purchase. The USDA has tracked the amount we spend on food as a proportion to our income, and that proportion has declined dramatically since 1960. The average share of per capita income spent on food fell from 17.0 percent in 1960 to 9.7 percent in 2014.[2]

In fact, Americans spend the lowest percent of consumer expenditures spent on food consumed at home compared to any other country in the world. According to the USDA Economic Research Service data, about 36 percent of household consumer expenditures in Egypt and Peru went to food consumed at home in 2014, compared with just 6.5 percent in the United States. Even the French and the Japanese spend double what we spend on food for home consumption—13.5 and 13.6 percent of all consumer expenditures respectively.

As someone who has dedicated his career to producing food, I take pride in this assurance of an abundant food supply that the American farmer has created for consumers in this country. Farmers have done such a good job of producing food that people have grown to expect a continuous, abundant food supply available at an affordable price. Farmers have also provided a high quality, nutritious, and safe food supply to consumers in this country and around the world.

Farming is in your blood. It's not just an occupation but a way of life. Growing up on a farm instilled in me a passion for the land and for planting a seed and watching it grow and produce more seed and for caring for livestock. I like being involved and getting things done and enjoy working with others to make that happen. It's difficult to get started in farming unless you have some connection. I always wanted to be a farmer, but with several uncles working with my dad and grandpa and my brothers also wanting to farm, little opportunity was left for me.

I wasn't sure if I would ever get the chance to farm. Then on a Sunday morning in April 1963 opportunity came knocking on my door. When I opened the door, I found my aunt Dorothy standing on the other side. She had come up to our house to see if I could feed the cattle for my uncle Clyde. He was having back problems and was in no condition to do his chores and needed help feeding his four hundred head of cattle. Of course, I agreed to help.

After I had finished the chores, I stopped by to talk to Uncle Clyde. Once the recap of the chores was complete, he shocked me by asking if I might be interested in farming with him. I didn't have to think twice about that and instantly said that I was. He was close to sixty years old at the time, and he and Aunt Dorothy had two daughters—Betty Jean and Kay. Neither one of which was interested in the farm.

Betty Jean and Kay both had degrees from the University of Illinois. They were both very successful and were married to men who had careers not related to farming. Betty Jean married Dr. David Wade, who had a PhD in nuclear engineering. Kay married Gordon Rednour, who had a master's degree in foreign economics and worked for the Ford Motor Company all of his life.

Since the husbands had no desire to farm, this created opportunity for me.

Uncle Clyde and Aunt Dorothy made me a deal that was very beneficial to me. They were very hard and sometimes almost cold businesspeople, but they taught me a lot about how to run a successful business. They agreed to sell me all the farm machinery and tools over a period of time. We decided upon a value of $7,200. A note was written, and I signed it saying that I would make a payment to them at 6 percent interest for seven years.

They also agreed to loan me the money each fall to buy calves. We would buy the calves at about four hundred pounds and feed them grass, hay, and corn for around a year to fifteen months and sell them to a processer at around twelve hundred pounds. When I sold the cattle, I would pay them for the cost of the calves plus 6 percent interest.

I made a payment to them on the fifteenth day of October for seven years at their home at noon. Aunt Dorothy was a very structured lady, and when she said noon she did not mean seven in the morning, and she didn't mean five minutes late, she meant that check was to be there at twelve o'clock on the dot.

I remember one time I had something else scheduled on October 15 at noon, so I went to make my payment in the morning. When I got to the door, Aunt Dorothy said that it was not due until noon and to come back then. Well I changed my plans and went back at noon and made the payment. That's the way Aunt Dorothy and Uncle Clyde were. They wanted things precise and to the point.

I also realized that I needed to ensure that I would be able to farm the land to make this work over the long term. In 1969 I made my last payment to Aunt Dorothy and Uncle Clyde for the machinery at precisely noon on the fifteenth day of October. After I handed over the check I asked them about buying the farm. Uncle Clyde did not think I could ever pay for it and was hesitant to see me borrow all that money. Aunt Dorothy reminded him that his dad was also hesitant when Uncle Clyde bought the 240 acres

I now live on. Uncle Clyde told me that when he bought the farm from Northwestern Mutual Life Insurance Company in 1938, he also bought a load of heifer calves, and they helped pay for the farm when he sold them.

Uncle Clyde and Aunt Dorothy agreed to sell me the farm but did not want to begin the transaction until 1972. One thing I knew for sure was that when Clyde and Dorothy Bradshaw told you something, you could etch it in stone. We started talking about establishing the price and terms for the land. They were exceptionally good to me with those provisions, although the price was a little higher than most land had been selling for. A neighbor's farm had just sold for $292 per acre, and that is what I agreed to pay for all of the 550 acres.

Aunt Dorothy and Uncle Clyde had a contract for deed drawn up that required only $10,000 down payment and twenty-eight years to pay off the farm. A payment would be made in the amount of $12,000 on the fifteenth day of October every year for twenty-eight years. The First National Bank of Pittsfield would hold the contract, and I would make the payments directly to the bank. That's exactly what I did, and true to her form every year for twenty-eight years, Aunt Dorothy would call the bank at five minutes after one to make sure I had made my payment. I think she really wanted to put that money on interest as fast as she could. In the eighties it was difficult to make those payments, but it was a big advantage to have the interest locked in at 6 percent when all the banks were charging 18 percent and sometimes as high as 21 percent interest. Although Aunt Dorothy and Uncle Clyde were very strict, I am forever grateful to them for giving me an opportunity to farm.

It's amazing for me to stop and think about all the advancements I have witnessed in farming from the time I was a boy growing up on our farm through my fifty-plus years of farming. These advances in agriculture have helped produce more food with fewer resources, which has benefited consumers in this country and around the world.

In 1963 when I started farming full time, our main crops were corn, oats, wheat, and grass to feed the cattle. The typical yields for our crops at that time were seventy-five to eighty bushels per acre for corn and thirty to forty bushels per acre for oats and wheat. The corn yields were quite an increase from when my dad had started farming in 1932. At that time the average corn yield was about forty bushels per acre. New hybrid seed corn helped make corn yields go up more rapidly than wheat and oats.

Controlling weeds has always been a problem for farmers over the years. Weeds can choke out the crops and cause them to yield less due to the competition for moisture and sunlight. We have made great strides in just this area alone. When my dad started farming, the only way he had to control weeds was by mechanical means. In the fall or early spring all the ground would be plowed with a moldboard plow turning all the vegetation under the ground to kill the weeds. Then in the spring, the ground would be disked, sometimes several times, to kill the weeds again and prepare the seedbed and then harrowed to smooth the ground before planting.

With no herbicides in those days, you only planted corn at 8,000 to 10,000 seeds to the acre, compared to today's population of 35,000 to 40,000 seeds per acre. Corn was usually planted sometime in the middle of May until early June. The corn was planted with a two-row horse-drawn planter and used what was called a "check wire." There would be a wire stretched all the way across the field, and it would be marked every forty inches. When this wire tripped the planter, it would drop one or two kernels of corn in the ground.

Corn being planted with a trip-wire planter in the 1940s. (Photo courtesy of Library of Congress—Farm Security Administration—Office of War Information Photograph Collection.)[3]

This was done so you could cultivate the corn in both directions to kill the weeds after the corn had sprouted and was growing in the field.

A horse-drawn cultivator was used to cut the weeds off between the corn and cover the weeds up with dirt around the corn.

Tilling the fields in the fall and spring and cultivating the corn in the summer took a lot of time. All this tillage loosened the soil and kept it bare for most of the year, so when it rained, it would wash the soil away. Farmers didn't know any better at the time, but looking back we lost a substantial amount of soil during those so-called good ol' days.

In 1945 the herbicide 2,4-D came on the market to help control weeds. With the use of 2,4-D, farmers no longer needed to check plant their corn. They could plant corn in rows rather than a checkerboard pattern and could plant more seeds per acre. No more stringing the wire and no more cultivating four times in both directions; just spray the corn fields with 2,4-D herbicide to kill the broadleaf weeds. Farmers would still cultivate to kill the grass between the rows of corn. The shovels were made so they would throw soil up around the corn stalk to cover the grass. This was called "laying corn by." Throughout most of the Midwest, farmers wanted this done by the Fourth of July because the corn would be too tall to cultivate after that time.

As a kid, I can remember Dad having an old Willys Jeep to spray corn. This jeep was made famous for its use in World War II. Mass numbers of these jeeps were produced for the war effort and helped transport soldiers and supplies in a variety of terrains and climates. It proved to be a reliable vehicle on the battlefield as well as the cornfield. We would set a one-hundred-gallon tank with a gasoline motor and pump in the back of the jeep and put a twelve-foot-wide spray boom on the front of the jeep and spray 2,4-D on all the cornfields.

Dad had several different jeeps over the years. Not only were they used to spray the corn, but as a teenager they were my principal means of transportation of an evening out on the town. I remember one particular night when driving our 1956 jeep to Perry, Illinois, became the news of the town. Perry is a little community of about six hundred people with businesses on both sides of a very wide street that I would estimate was probably one hundred feet wide with a bandstand in the middle. In 1956 dad got a new jeep, and one of my friend's family had a new Chevrolet car. Being teenage boys, we began debating whose vehicle would be the fastest. Of course, there was only one way to truly figure it out—a drag race.

On the night of the big race a number of people gathered on the streets of Perry to watch our Willys Jeep go up against the new Chevrolet power shift car. It was a fun evening although frowned upon by some, but most in town enjoyed the show. I knew my jeep had four-wheel-drive and a very short movement to shift between gears and a good clutch, meaning I could shift faster than the automatic transmission in the Chevrolet. The distance was only a little over the length of a football field. Also, there was loose gravel on the street, so my four-wheel-drive jeep would have better traction.

When the young man that was the designated starter dropped the flag, I trounced on the gas and shifted as fast as I could. The little Willys Jeep outran the Chevrolet and won the drag race. It had proved to be a versatile vehicle useful as a winner not only on the battlefield but also on the drag strip and reliable in the farm fields.

By the time that I started farming in 1963, another new chemical had been developed that helped control grasses in corn—Atrazine. We sprayed Atrazine in a ten- to twelve-inch band over the corn rows to kill the grass in the row of corn. Corn is part of the grass family, so prior to Atrazine it was difficult to kill the grass and not the corn. At that time, we planted about fifteen thousand seeds per acre in thirty-eight-inch rows.

To help further control the weeds and to get a soft seedbed, we would plow with a moldboard plow and then drag the soil with a harrow and hope and pray for a rain to firm the soil back up. Then we went into the field and disked the ground sometimes three or four times to get the ground smooth and all the weeds covered up. Then we would harrow the ground again and finally plant with a four-row planter.

After the corn came up and was about three inches tall, we would spray Atrazine over top of the rows and 2,4-D across all of the ground. Then we would cultivate between the rows of corn to get rid of any remaining grass and weeds and hope they did not grow back before the corn got tall enough to shade between the rows.

Fast forward fifty-three years to the time when my grandson is starting to farm. Those same fields that we used to till several times a year are planted with minimal cultivation and in some cases no cultivation. We no longer even own a moldboard plow and do very little disking or harrowing.

For raising corn, we use a field cultivator that doesn't turn the soil over to help prepare the seedbed right before we plant.

Today's planters can have up to forty-eight rows, which is 120 feet wide. They are capable of folding down to a size that can be safely transported on a road. Modern planters can plant 32,000 to 45,000 corn seeds per acre and with simple adjustments can go from planting corn to planting 90,000 to 150,000 soybean seeds per acre. On our farm we plant corn with a twelve-row planter in thirty-inch rows at thirty-five thousand seeds per acre. Modern planters allow seeds to be planted into soil covered by last year's crop residue. The heavy ground cover left by last year's crops helps keep down weed germination and growth, which lowers the need for herbicides.

The tractor and planter utilize GPS technology to ensure that the seeds are planted with precision. Sensors on the planter count the seeds dropped in each row and relay how many seeds per acre are being planted along with the depth the seed is planted to a computer monitor in the tractor. This monitor can also vary the seeding rate based on multiple layers of information such as the past yield data, soil fertility levels, and overall production potential. The technology also allows the planter to turn off each row as you come to the end of the field or an area you do not want to plant.

A modern John Deere twenty-four-row corn planter can plant approximately forty acres of corn in one hour. (© Illinois Agricultural Association, 2018. Used with permission.)

We spray the corn early in the spring and then again when the corn is up and growing. We use far less chemicals by keeping the weeds from going to seed and get much better weed control. Some chemicals we only use a few ounces per acre of the product compared to many gallons per acre in the past. The sprayers now use GPS and auto steering and automatically shut off when reaching a part of the field that has already been sprayed. This technology helps reduce the amount of chemicals that we use, which saves us money and is better for the environment.

We have always used livestock manure on our fields as fertilizer. In the early days we spread it on top of the ground, but today the manure is injected into the ground six to eight inches deep before the corn is planted. We also use commercial fertilizer to provide nitrogen, phosphorus, and potassium on some of our fields. Corn yields in the same fields that used to be 75 bushels per acre are now 175 to 200 bushels per acre.

In 1964 we planted the first soybeans on this farm. Many farmers in central Illinois and around the country had been planting soybeans for many years. My grandfather raised soybeans back in the '30s as a high-protein feedstuff for his cows to graze or to put up as hay. We raised our soybeans much like we did our corn. We moldboard plowed the field, dragged it, disked it, harrowed it, and then planted. We planted in thirty-eight-inch rows and cultivated the soybeans normally two times and then walked through and cut the weeds out with a hoe later in the summer. Walking soybean fields was a hot, hard job. A forty-acre field looked mighty big when you had to walk every row. The first soybeans in 1964 made just less than thirty bushels to the acre, which was about what the county averaged.

Today, many soybeans are planted with no cultivation at all. On our farm, soybeans are planted with a no-till split row planter where the rows are only fifteen inches apart and will shade the weeds out very quickly. We spray herbicide over all the ground before we plant early in the spring so no weeds will grow up and then we spray one time after the soybeans are growing. The soybeans on the same field that made less than thirty bushels to the acre in the 1960s now make fifty-five to sixty bushels per acre.

It frustrates me when people want farming to go back to the ways of the past, thinking that it would be better for the environment or our health or society as a whole. Trust me, I grew up in those times, and I wouldn't want to go back to canning our own food, processing our own livestock, or milking our own cow.

I don't know too many people that want to go back to driving around in a Model T for their daily transportation or would give up using their computers for their jobs or personal life. Farming, like many other industries, has changed greatly in part by the utilization of technology. These changes have led to improvements in how we produce our food with increases in production and benefits to the environment.

Hopefully as we move into the future, our society will not allow fear-mongering to convince them that advancements in food production are a negative thing and instead will embrace these new ag technologies and see the benefits that they are producing.

Marrying Linda and Joining the Army

Sharing your life with someone you love and who loves you is one of the most rewarding and fulfilling parts of your life. As I look back on my life there are many rewarding experiences that I have had the opportunity to be a part of, but all of those pale in comparison to marrying Linda. I have made many decisions along my life's journey—some good and some not so good, but without a doubt the best decision I ever made was asking Linda to marry me.

In the spring of 1960, I asked Linda to be my wife (and she said yes). I don't remember my proposal being a huge romantic ordeal. I just knew that she was the one for me, and I wanted to spend the rest of my life with her. Linda had helped improve my grades in college, so I thought that was a good sign that she was a keeper. With our engagement and pending wedding, I wanted to try to graduate from college as soon as I could. To help speed this process along, I decided to take summer classes. I had been motivated to do well in college, but now I was really motivated.

I also looked for additional opportunities to earn some money to start building up some savings to support my soon-to-be wife. I began working part time in the winter of 1960 for the Illinois Department of Agriculture to run tests on semitruck loads of hogs. The department was trying to determine how to prevent the loss of tissue weight in pigs when they were shipped to processing plants. Pigs would typically lose 2 to 3 percent of their body weight when they were loaded on a truck and shipped to market before they were processed. This loss in weight was losing the farmer money and also meant less pork for the consumer. Anything that could help reduce the weight loss would help both groups.

As part of this job, I would go to HighGrade Stockyards in Bushnell, Illinois, just a few miles from Macomb, where I would divide a semitruck load of hogs into equal groups. Usually the truck would hold around 172 to 180 hogs each weighing 225 to 240 pounds. I fed half the hogs brown sugar and water before they were loaded on the truck, and the other half received just water.

The idea behind feeding the pigs brown sugar water was to try to increase the sugar in the bloodstream and thus in the meat. The theory was that more sugar in the meat would mean less breakdown of the muscle tissues in the hams, loins, and other cuts of pork. The less breakdown of the muscle tissues would result in more meat. The pigs were trucked to a plant in Indianapolis that processed twelve thousand pigs a day, which I believe was one of the biggest plants in the United States at that time.

I would ride along in the semitruck headed to Indianapolis, and we would arrive usually sometime around midnight. They would start taking the pigs to the processing plant the next morning a little before six o'clock, so it was a short night. As the pigs were unloaded off the truck, I would tattoo each pig to identify and track which pig had been fed the brown sugar water and which one had not. After the pigs were slaughtered, I would write down the weight of each carcass. Then I would wait twenty-four hours and take another weight when the carcasses were hanging in the cooler. After several trials, the data showed that there was a little less weight loss in the meat from the pigs fed the brown sugar water, but not enough to make it a common industry practice.

With having to wait twenty-four hours between taking weight samples of the carcass, I had a lot of time on my hands. The plant manager, Mr. Dierks, was a very influential and busy man around Indianapolis. I got to know him pretty well with all the trips I made to the plant. He would often find interesting things for me to do during my down time.

He was on the hospital board of directors and decided that it would be a good experience for me to spend an afternoon and evening at the emergency room in Indianapolis. He thought it would be interesting for me to see what a big city hospital was like. He offered to make some phone calls and got the details arranged.

It was quite an experience for a country boy to see all the patients that came into the emergency room. One man walked in with a knife stuck in his stomach and a lady came in to have a baby and ended up having the baby right as she walked in the door. Another time he arranged for me to drive my new Chevrolet Biscayne six-cylinder, two-door, AM radio, one-sun-visor car around the Indianapolis 500 Raceway! That was something that I never will forget.

During the early 1960s, the Cold War was heating up. The threat of nuclear Armageddon was a constant discussion topic in the news. To reduce the threat of nuclear war, the US foreign policy was to contain any expansion of communism around the globe. This meant the US military needed an increase in personnel to be ready for a fight that might pop up anywhere around the world. For young men my age this meant the likely event that you would be called into service. The Cuban missile crisis under President Kennedy forced me to take action.

Throughout 1960, I was aware that my name was getting close to the top of the list in Pike County to be drafted into the military. In December I went to Scott Air Force Base, located close to St. Louis, and applied for the air force. A recruiter had assured me that if I joined and already had my college degree, I could be a pilot even though I wore glasses. I took a written exam that the air force gave me and passed, so I thought I had it made. However, I had one more test to pass. They put me in a little chair and spun me around three or four times and then told me to get up and walk a straight line. As soon as I got out of the chair I was stumbling and wobbling around like I was drunk. I couldn't walk a straight line to save my life, so they did not want me to fly their planes. After this I decided I would wait for the draft.

I completed college on March 3, 1961, and then went back in May to go through the graduation ceremonies. Upon completing college, I needed to get a full-time job. My father knew some men who had started a new insurance company. They were looking for a life insurance salesman. The position was commissions only but sounded like an opportunity to make some decent money, where the more effort that I put into my work, the more money that I could make. I started with Investors Security Life Insurance Company in March 1961.

There were only two positive things that I gained from that job. The number one thing I learned from this selling position was how to make presentations and how to get people to sign on the dotted line. They sent me for a two-week sales training class, which was taught by some very professional and very talented businesspeople such as Earl Nightingale and Clement Stone. Mr. Stone was supposedly the wealthiest man in Illinois at the time and was a hotshot salesman in the insurance business.

We went through practice sessions on how to make a sales presentation. I call them canned presentations, as you said the same thing time after time, but they did work. We were taught to always end the conversation for the sale with, "Do you want a policy with an option or without an option?" If the customer said, as most or a lot of them did, "without the option," we wrote up the policy that way, and if they said "with the option," we wrote up the policy with the option. Either way we sold a life insurance policy, so it was a little bit of a trick on words, but it was a very effective approach.

I did meet some good people who were in the training class with me, such as Vince Demuzio. Vince went on to become a state senator from our area and to be the chairman of the Democratic Party in Illinois. I had the opportunity to work with Vince on several occasions.

The second positive thing I gained from this job was that I did make a lot of money right out of college. I worked as an insurance salesman for eighteen months and made a little under $60,000. This job was one of the few things I ever did that I look back on and do not feel proud about doing. I sold many of my friends and relatives an insurance policy that never did what the company said it would do. The insurance policies did not make the money we were all led to believe they would make for the policy owners. That was my only job in my life that was not directly tied to agriculture.

Linda and I got married on July 2, 1961, and Linda Bradburn officially became Linda Bradshaw. The little Christian church in Detroit, Illinois, where we had the ceremony did not have air conditioning, and it was hotter than hell in the church. Thankfully no one passed out due to the heat. We headed west on a two-week honeymoon to Yellowstone National Park, the Black Hills, and through Colorado. We did come home a little early because I had a big insurance sale pending in Mount Sterling.

Right before our wedding, I was able to accomplish a personal financial goal. I paid off my loan at the Farmers National Bank. I had owed that bank money since 1955 when I took out my first loan at age sixteen to buy twelve pigs to finish out for my 4-H project. My debt freedom didn't last very long. I had to borrow more money when I got home from our honeymoon to feed a few pigs I still had with dad and my younger brother, Harvey. Those twelve days of our honeymoon were the only time since I was sixteen that I have not owed the Farmers National Bank money. Over the years my most important relationship has always been with Linda, but my banker would be a close second!

From the beginning of our marriage, Linda and I learned to be frugal with our money. We were saving as much of the money from my insurance job as we could. I had dreams of farming full time, and I knew that I would need a lot of money to start farming. We lived our first year of marriage in rented houses and scraped by on five dollars a week for groceries and miscellaneous expenses. Even in those days that was not much money to live on, but somehow we made it work. The old saying is true: "What money can't buy, love can get you through."

In November 1961, I was only two or three names away from the top of the draft list in Pike County, so I decided rather than take my chances on getting drafted, I would go ahead and enlist in the army reserves and go for six months active duty and serve six years in the reserves. I went to basic training in Fort Leonard Wood, Missouri, in April 1962. Not too long before I left, we found out we were going to have our first baby in October. I was a little anxious about leaving Linda during her first pregnancy, but I had already committed to serve my country.

While I was gone for my six months of active duty, Linda lived with her parents, Vernon and Aleen Bradburn. My father-in-law rented 140 acres and my mother-in-law's family owned one hundred acres and this was all the land that they farmed. They farmed much differently than the way my family farmed. Their farm was owned by two ministers from Indiana, and everything was split 50-50 including the crops, hogs, and cattle. They had a good life but did not have a lot of extra money. They took good care of Linda while I was gone, and that helped ease my mind about being away from her.

It didn't take me long to realize that I did not like the army. It's not that I had any major issues or problems; I just did not like the structured atmosphere and always being told what to do. I was twenty-two at the time and a little older than most of the other guys in my company. There were a couple other guys like me who were college graduates and did not take an officer commission. The rest were just out of high school. Thankfully I was in good shape, so the training was not exceptionally hard for me. I remember that I did not lose or gain much weight during my service.

Being in the army did not hinder my entrepreneurial spirit. I was always looking for an opportunity to make a few extra dollars. The army was tearing down some old barracks on the base that had been built back during World War II and was replacing them with more modern facilities. The barracks were two-story buildings made out of yellow pine. The lumber was still in pretty good shape. A guy by the name of Smirtcheck had started tearing down the barracks to salvage the lumber. When I got off duty I helped him and was paid $1 per hour.

The commanding officer had told Smirtcheck that he needed to get a bond to be officially hired to do the job, but he wasn't able to come up with enough money for the bond, so he had to quit working on the project. When I went home for a weekend for a short leave, I took some of the boards to show my dad and Uncle Clyde. They said that they could use the lumber around the farm and would be able to sell as much of the lumber as I could get.

When I got back to the base, I asked the officer in charge if we posted the bond could we finish tearing down some of the barracks and keep the lumber. He agreed, and Dad posted a $100,000 bond so Smirtcheck was legal and could get back to work. He would drop the buildings, and then I and some of my army buddies would tear the boards apart. We worked on this for several months and ended up getting five livestock trailer semitruck loads of lumber. We used a couple of loads around the farm for building projects and sold the other loads. I made a couple thousand dollars on the project.

One day during basic training the company commanding officer came to our platoon and asked if anyone had any carpentry experience. I raised my hand. He immediately took me across the base in a jeep to the ball diamonds. A set of wooden bleachers needed to be fixed from the damage caused by a truck backing into them. He asked if I could repair them, and I said that I thought I could. I got three or four of my buddies to help me, and we were allowed to work on the bleachers while the rest of the company practiced marching. We dragged out the project as long as we could to miss as much marching as possible. I could never stay in step very well, so my commanding officers usually let me out of the marches going by the review stands.

One thing I did excel at in the army was hand-to-hand combat training. I can thank three drunk guys from Pittsfield who helped me in this area.

For many years Griggsville was a dry town, selling no alcohol in the town limits. This was the case during my high school days. It has only been within the last few years that voters passed an ordinance allowing alcohol to be sold in the town. Before that time everyone who wanted alcohol would go to Valley City, Pittsfield, or Meredosia. Valley City was a little town of just seventeen people four miles east of Griggsville. Despite their small population, there were always two taverns until one of them burned down. The ironic thing was that voters passed an ordinance making Valley City dry at the same time Griggsville voted to allow alcohol.

The fact that I lived in a dry town really wasn't a problem for me. I never drank a drop of alcohol until I was out of high school. When I got out of high school, like a lot of young men and women, I finally tried alcohol. The August before I went to college, I had two beers with some of my buddies. Nothing too wild and crazy. Then I went to the Cardinal Inn in Pittsfield to get something to eat. I thought I had enough to drink. Three boys from Pittsfield were in the restaurant who were drunk.

They came over to where I was sitting in a booth and told me to get out of town. They were smoking and put their cigarettes out in my food. I didn't want to start any trouble, and I could tell the odds of three against one were not in my favor, so I got up and left. I went home and never said a word to anyone about what happened. I was disappointed that I didn't stand up and defend myself. That night has been something that I have never forgotten, and it made a lasting impact on me. The encounter made me realize that you always have to be prepared for the unexpected, and you can't be prepared when you excessively drink alcohol. From that point on, I never drank but a small amount of alcohol at any one time in my life.

Although it was a bad experience, I learned a lot of lessons from it. I don't want to sound like I hold grudges, but I had the opportunity to keep the ringleader of that group from getting a job on two different occasions. Sometimes justice does come to those that wait. The experience also helped me get interested in learning a sport that would come in very handy in my future!

The first thing I did at WIU, after I got my classes lined up, was sign up for the judo club. A man by the name of Davis, who was an employee at the time with the Postal Service in Peoria, came to campus once a week and held judo classes. Mr. Davis had been in the service during World War II and trained in hand-to-hand combat and sport judo during and after the war in Japan while serving in the occupation forces. I remained in that judo club throughout my three and a half years at Western.

I was never the top student in the judo class, but I was good enough that by my junior and senior years I conducted and held the class during the times that Mr. Davis was not there. A college math professor took lessons with me. He was a veteran who had served during World War II and had been interested in judo. The head of the agriculture department at the time, Dr. John McVickar, also took some lessons. I progressed through my judo training and was awarded a first-degree black belt in sport judo. Our club would put on demonstrations, and we went to Chicago for competition matches. It was a great experience that boosted my self-confidence and taught me some valuable skills that would be worthwhile in my days in the army.

During my basic training, the drill sergeants had us all psyched up for the combat training. The trainees were taking turns practicing hand-to-hand combat with our sergeant, who was annihilating the trainees one by one. I stood and watched him make the same move every time, and every time he was victorious over his opponent. He was really hitting the guys hard.

At five feet five and 140 pounds soaking wet, I didn't look like I stood a chance against this six-foot two-hundred-pound sturdy sergeant. I know he was overlooking me when I stepped up to him. The sergeant came at me and attempted to use the same move on me that he had been successful with on the other trainees. This time it ended in a much different way for him as I quickly put him on the ground. He was shocked and upset that he had been defeated, but he did appreciate the fact that I had received some training that was valuable. After proving myself worthy in the area of hand-to-hand combat, I did help with some of the training throughout my military career. However, as with anything in life, you are never good enough to not fail. On two occasions, I was beaten up pretty badly. One of the trainees hit me really hard, and I went down instantly. I received a bad bruise on my lower abdomen and was laid up for several days. This was one time that I was glad I wasn't taller, as the blow would have been right in this private's privates!

I spent six months on active duty, and then from 1962 to 1968 I was in the reserves, which required attending weekly meetings, weekend trainings, and two weeks of training every summer. I was in an 81 mm mortar team in the reserves. This was a small hand-carried mortar used extensively in World War II. By 1965 the military was having a big buildup for the Vietnam War. Two reserve units were based out of Quincy, Illinois. In August 1965, President Lyndon Johnson activated one of the Quincy reserve units. Luckily for me, I was in the one that was not called up, and I did not have to go to Vietnam.

My service in the army reserves was a very hectic time of my life. Our daughter, Cindy, was born on October 31, 1962, two weeks after I got home from my active-duty service. I started farming full time in the spring of 1963, while also doing some student teaching. We had purchased a little house in town in 1962 but then moved to the farm in October 1965 where my aunt and uncle had lived. This is still the same house that we live in today. Then our second daughter, Lisa, was born on June 8, 1966.

As a farmer, taking two weeks off every summer to go to reserve training was sometimes a challenge. It always seemed like there was something that needed to be done on the farm during the time that I had to be away at reserves. One year the company had to go in June. I hadn't finished planting the crops and received a deferment to go in late July or early August. In the summer of 1963 I was baling alfalfa hay and putting it in the barns at the same time my uncle had someone combining oats. We were putting the oats in the bin on the west side of the barn next to where we were putting the hay. I was to leave for training in a few days, so I wanted to get all the hay baled and oats harvested before I left for two weeks.

I was unloading the wagons of hay onto the elevator that was taking the bales up in the barn. When the wagons were empty and headed back to the field to get another load, I started scooping oats off the truck into the bin until the wagons arrived with another load of hay. I did this nonstop for several hours. It was so hot that I got overheated, and my younger brother, Harvey, put me in his air-conditioned car and took me to the doctor. The doctor told me to stay in air-conditioning for two or three days and gave me something to drink. I made it just fine, but it took two days to recover, and I was late going to training.

Being in the reserves was difficult, but for those of us who were farmers, it was that much more demanding. The weekend trainings started at eight in the morning in Quincy, which was a one-hundred-mile round trip for me. That meant those of us with livestock had to get up at four in the morning and do our chores so we could leave at seven to be there by eight. The training usually lasted until five in the evening, then we would drive home Saturday night and do our chores. I would get up on Sunday and do the whole thing over again. Those were long, hard weekends.

I remember scooping snow in the dark out of the pens in front of the hog sheds to have a place to feed the sows with little pigs. You find out who your friends are when you get into that kind of work. Jim Dennison was my feed salesman who sold King Feed. On a number of occasions, Jim came to the farm and helped me do my chores before I left for reserves. He helped ensure that my hogs and cattle were properly cared for and went above and beyond the duty of a feed salesman. Looking back on those years when we were first married, I'm not sure that Linda and I could have handled anything more. Like any good marriage, the tough times have made our relationship even stronger and after fifty-eight years of marriage I can still say I'm glad I married my best friend.

Phil and Linda at a Fighting Illini Pork Club event in 2015. (Photo courtesy of Phil Bradshaw.)

Tragedy Helps Refocus My Life

Traveling is something I have always enjoyed. Getting to see new and interesting places, meeting different people, and experiencing new things is all part of the adventure. My travels began at an early age, even before my big trip to Mexico. Probably not many people can say that they traveled to New York City by themselves as a teenager, but I did.

My cousin, Margaret Myers, who was thirteen years older than me, had moved to New York City and was a nurse at a hospital on the east side of Manhattan along the East River. She invited me to come visit her. It was 1955, and I was sixteen years old. The thought of going to New York City was amazing, but I never thought my parents would approve. We were not able to afford for my parents to go with me, so I knew the only way that I could go would be on my own.

To my surprise, not only did my parents approve, they also purchased the airplane and train tickets for me to go. Since Margaret let me stay in her apartment, all I had to do was save money for my miscellaneous expenses. I worked around the farm putting up hay and doing other jobs the summer before and that summer. I also cleaned an old building where they showed movies three or four nights a week. I had a few show pigs that I sold and got a little money from them.

We purchased my airplane ticket to fly from St. Louis, Missouri, to New York City. I was definitely excited, and I'll admit I was a little bit nervous to be traveling on my own, headed to the largest city in the country. This was also my first plane ride, so that added to my excitement and nervousness. It was an interesting experience, but still to this day I don't really understand why my parents let me get on that plane all by myself as a teenage boy to go to New York City, but they did.

My mother insisted that I wear a suit and tie to travel, but I think the airline actually required men to dress in a suit or at least a sports jacket. I wasn't crazy about the attire, but it did make me feel important. My folks walked me right to the plane and helped me find my seat. There were no TSA security checks back in those days! I remember being anxious as the plane taxied down the runaway and lifted off. Once in the air at our cruising altitude, I relaxed and enjoyed the ride. It took a little more than four and a half hours to make the flight to New York.

When I landed in New York, Margaret and her friend, Roseanne, who was also a nurse, met me at the airport. I stayed in their small apartment, which was on the fifth floor, and their building did not have an elevator. The entire apartment wasn't much bigger than just a couple rooms of my house. There was not a lot of personal space.

I stayed for eight days. I arrived the last week of July and traveled home on the train the fifth and sixth of August. We did all the usual New York City tourist things such as visit Radio City Music Hall, go to the Empire State Building, attend a theater on Fifth Avenue, walk through Times Square, and much more. We also went to Coney Island, where I rode the rides with Margaret and Roseanne. We visited the Statue of Liberty, and I can remember walking up all the steps.

The trip included many firsts for my life. One of which was seeing the ocean for the first time. It was amazing to see the water disappear into the horizon. It wasn't just enough to see the ocean; Margaret insisted that we get in and go swimming.

Now I have never been a very good swimmer and have always had a slight fear of the water. This can be traced back to a tragic event that happened at the swimming hole at my grandfather's creek. The Griggsville Methodist Church had a swim party for junior high children. There were no swimming pools in the area, so everyone would swim in a creek, river, or in one of the few ponds that were deep enough. The Sunday school class went to my grandfather's creek to a favorite swimming hole called "Rock Ledge." I was not there that day, but my older brother, Fred, was. No one knows exactly how it happened, but a young boy drowned that afternoon in the swimming hole. There were adults there as well, and many of them were good swimmers. It was just one of those things that happened that no one could explain. It was such a tragedy, and it happened at a place where I had been many times. This event made me afraid of the water for the rest of my life.

Flash forward to the Atlantic Ocean and me a sixteen-year-old boy swimming with two older girls. I was trying to show off and not show any fear. I tried diving through one of the waves, but I soon found myself being pulled farther away from the shore. I tried to swim back, but the undertow was too strong. I began to panic, which is never a good thing to do in the water. Luckily for me, Margaret was able to rescue me and pull me back to shore. No damage done, just a little pride lost.

Another first was going to see a television program being produced. I think the program was called *Chance of a Lifetime*. Our family did not have a TV, but I had watched television at one of our neighbor's homes. Mr. Kopps lived in Griggsville and was part owner of the Trio Manufacturing Company, which produced TV antennas at that time. His son, Lawrence, was two years older than me. I would stop by their house and watch their TV that they bought in 1952. Some people in our community purchased televisions in 1955 or 1956, but we did not buy one until 1957. It was interesting to get a behind-the-scenes look of a TV show and everything that went into making it happen.

After eight days it was time for me to head back home. Margaret and Roseanne took me to Grand Central Station and put me on a train heading for St. Louis. I sat by three older ladies; they were probably only in their fifties, but at the time that was old to me. You could buy food on the train, but it was expensive. I had brought a couple of apples to eat, but the ladies had packed all kinds of food. They insisted that I eat with them, and being a hungry teenage boy, I didn't protest. They helped make the trip back home go by quickly, except all three of the ladies snored loudly as the train traveled through the night.

Overall it was a great trip and quite an experience for a sixteen-year-old Midwest boy. The thing that had the biggest impact on me was that it opened my eyes to the huge population that needed to be fed. While we were in New York City we went to a grocery store. I was amazed at all the food choices. It was remarkable to think about how all that food got produced, processed, and transported from all across the country to be available to all the people in the city. It made me appreciate more my family's role in producing food for a growing population and made me realize that the hard work on the farm was an important part of the larger society.

This experience would not have been possible if not for my parents allowing me to go and helping me get there. My parents, like many parents, wanted their children to have a better life than they had and have opportunities that they didn't have. This was apparent in the trips that I was able to take as a teenager—New York City at age sixteen and Mexico at age twenty—compared to my parents who had traveled very little.

My parents were thrifty as were many in their generation who had lived through the Great Depression. I don't ever remember thinking that we were poor or never having what we needed, but I realize now how hard my mother and father worked and how much they sacrificed for their kids.

Dad would work hard all day long, and we would not see him from dawn to dusk as he tended to the livestock and the crops that Grandpa had. Mother worked hard to take care of me and my brothers. Keeping us fed and clean was a full-time job.

Mother raised chickens in an old chicken house where she had a few laying hens. My brothers and I would gather the eggs every day. Mother would get around forty small chicks each spring from a place in Pittsfield and raise them in a little cage on the back porch of our house. She would get the baby chicks so they would be ready to eat by the Fourth of July, when we celebrated not only our country's independence, but also the end of the planting season.

I can still remember helping my mother dress the chickens. Mother had a little tree stump that Dad had driven two nails in just the right distance apart to hold the chicken's head. Mother had a little ax that she used to very quickly remove the chicken's head. We would remove the guts and intestines and then steam the chickens in scalding water, which always smelled bad. Then we would pick the feathers off, and mother would cut the chicken up, and we would have fried chicken. This was a lot of work, but the chicken always tasted so good.

When I was younger, my parents didn't have their own vehicle. They used the old truck that Dad and Grandpa used to deliver coal to homes around Griggsville during the day and that was our family vehicle at night. I have fond memories of every Saturday night taking the old truck to Griggsville to get groceries. Dad and Mother would usually both go to the store and give the store owner a list of what they wanted. The owner or his helper would go around and put everything in paper bags and would even help you put them in the old truck. Sometimes Mother would have a few extra eggs that she would trade to the store for groceries. Other times Dad and Mother would leave the list with the grocery store and leave us boys in Griggsville while they went to Pittsfield, which was eight miles away, to sell the eggs.

I can remember riding in the back of that old truck with my two brothers and curling up under a blanket inside the spare tire. To this day, I don't understand how Mother kept us three boys looking so nice. During the day we played in the dirty chicken house and at night rode in the back of that old, dirty truck with black coal dust everywhere, but we always looked clean and nice thanks to Mother.

Mother dedicated her life to raising her three boys. She was always there for us to help us with anything, to comfort us in times of need, and to listen to the good and the bad. There are things that I would tell my mother that I would never tell anyone else. Mother was so focused on raising her three boys; she rarely did anything for herself. She was very proud of her family. Fred and I had graduated from college, and Harvey had completed a few years of college. We all three were married, and I had started a family of my own. My oldest daughter, Cindy, was three. Mother was finally to the point in her life where she was able to spend some time and energy on herself.

Then, tragically, in January 1966 my mother passed away at the age of fifty-two of spinal meningitis. At that time, she lived less than two miles up the road from me, but I had not talked to her in more than two weeks. My aunt Dorothy called me and my two brothers and told us we should go to the hospital in Quincy right away to see Mother. Unfortunately, she passed away before we made it to the hospital. Dad had taken her to the hospital only a few hours earlier.

This was definitely a real life changer for the whole family. To make matters worse, my older brother, Fred, had also lost his first wife, Joyce, a few months before. Joyce was one of the first fatalities of the birth control pill. Twenty-one months after she started taking the pill, she died suddenly. She was only twenty-three. She had hepatitis when she was younger, and doctors later determined that the birth control pill was lethal for people that had hepatitis.

It's been said that bad things usually happen in threes, and that was the case for our family. Linda's grandfather died in May 1965; Fred's wife died in September 1965, and Mother died in January 1966. Three family members' deaths in just nine months' time was a lot for us to handle.

Since she was so young, it was a shock to have lost Mother. There was so much that she and Dad had planned to do but had never taken the time. Dad had stayed on the farm all his life to help Grandpa pay off the large debt he had accumulated during the Great Depression. He and Mother had gone to Arizona to see Aunt Ethel and Uncle Royal a time or two, but that was the extent of their travels. The old house they were living in was modern but needed some work. They had been putting off traveling and repairing the house, and then mother passed away unexpectedly, and they never got to travel or to fix the house.

I was twenty-six when Mother passed away. Her death made quite an impression on me. I remember talking with Linda about how we didn't want to end up like my parents, waiting to do things that never happened. Mother's untimely death made me realize that I couldn't put off my dreams and plans, because tomorrow may never come. I decided that I would take every opportunity that I could to travel. I also wanted to get involved in ag organizations and help make a difference on the many issues and challenges facing agriculture.

I was reminded of that trip to New York City and the feeling of trying to feed all those people. I wanted to be in a position to help grow the food on the farm but also help grow the ag industry to meet the growing demand for food in this country and around the world.

I believe that you have to make the most of every situation, and in a way Mother's passing had forced me to refocus my life. I have often thought that I think Mother would be proud of all the things that her sons have accomplished, knowing that she helped us become the people that we are today.

8

Strength in Numbers

The idea that there is strength in numbers and that we, as a people, are stronger working together rather than individually has been proven to be true in numerous situations and circumstances. Usually a group of people working in unison has more influence or power than a person working alone. This is true in religion, politics, sports, business, and in many other settings. Strength in numbers helped our forefathers defeat the British Empire and gain our independence. The collective efforts of the Allies and the people back home helped win World War II.

Over the years, farmers have come together to initiate organizations and groups as needed to address challenges and issues. During World War II, the market for the fat from the pigs (called lard) was very strong because it was used to manufacture explosives. Most of the lard available in the United States was diverted for military purposes, so American consumers switched to vegetable oils for cooking. After the war, the demand for lard dropped greatly. People no longer wanted the fat from the pig to use for cooking, and synthetic and vegetable products replaced lard for industrial and military purposes. Farmers joined together to improve pig genetics with less fat and to develop better production practices and techniques for raising leaner pigs. Producers in Illinois started the Illinois Swine Herd Improvement Association to remain competitive and produce what consumers were demanding.

The Illinois Swine Herd Improvement Association later became the Illinois Pork Producers Association (IPPA) with similar objectives of helping farmers improve ways of raising pigs and promote pork to consumers. Most pork-producing states soon started an association to bring together producers to accomplish comparable missions. After several state organizations were formed, there was a need for a national organization.

A group of about one hundred pork producers from across the United States assembled in Moline, Illinois, in 1963 to start a national pork producer group. Those from Illinois who attended that meeting banded together and put up the money to hire Chuck Bloomberg as the first executive director of IPPA. Illinois had some great leaders who were very influential in starting the state and national pork groups. The ones that I worked with the most were: George Brauer, Russ Jeckel, Dutch Johnson, Gibb Fricke, Albert Gehlbach, Wilbur Paulus, Wayne Heberer, Wayne Maschhoff, Elmer Frazee, and Lindell Loveless. These are just a few of the ones that I can remember.

One of the biggest responsibilities at the beginning for the national pork organization was to educate and promote to farmers a national checkoff for hogs sold in the United States. A pilot project was started in Henry and Rock Island Counties in Illinois and Scott and Clinton Counties, which were directly across the Mississippi River in Iowa. The program was very simple. When a farmer sold a market pig, they were to contribute one nickel to the national pork organization. This was called "Nickels for Profit," and it went very well in those four pilot counties. In fact, the "Nickels for Profit" effort went so well that it was implemented across the country.

Farmers in leadership positions at the county, state, and national levels spent most of their time trying to get more farmers to agree to have a nickel taken out of their check for every hog sold. The buyer would then send the money to the National Pork Producers Council (NPPC) in Des Moines, Iowa, or to the state association. This meant that for the program to be successful, we also had to have the support of the many companies buying the pigs.

In the past, when pigs were ready for market, many farmers would haul them to the larger stockyards located in Chicago, St. Louis, or Kansas City. Recall the story of me riding with my uncle through Alton on the way to the stockyards in East St. Louis. Typically, these stockyards were located near large railroad yards, so that after the animals were processed, the meat could be shipped to markets around the country. The stockyards began to decline in the late 1950s as advancements in truck transportation and direct sales of livestock from farmers to packers made it cheaper to process animals closer to where they were raised. Several companies built pork processing plants throughout the Midwest during this time. This changed the way that hogs were marketed.

During the late 1960s, most hogs were being marketed at many different buying stations throughout the United States. A buying station was the middle man between the farmer and the packer. Interstate Producers Livestock Association was a part of the Illinois Farm Bureau and was one of the larger purchasers of hogs in the state of Illinois. Another major one in the Midwest was Heinold Hog Markets, headquartered in Indiana. Most major pork processors, such as Cargill, Hormel, Oscar Meyer, Swift, Tyson, and other plants also had buying stations throughout the country. There were also a number of small buyers across the Midwest that purchased pigs and resold them or just purchased them for the packer. The buying stations became common throughout the Midwest and most of the country where livestock was raised.

Over the years, farmers, especially those raising pigs, began to market their animals directly to the packers. Today, the majority of pigs are sold directly to the plants where they are processed. There are a few buying stations remaining, but there are a lot fewer than back in the 1960s.

When the "Nickels for Profit" was beginning, there were many market options for farmers. It was a very big job to contact all these markets and get everyone to hold money out of the farmers' checks to finance the NPPC. I traveled many miles to visit with the different markets, asking them to go on the implied consent program known as "Nickels for Profit." This program was set up for the buyer to deduct five cents for every pig marketed, unless the producer said no. This program worked well with some buyers and helped increase funding for the state and national pork producer organizations. About a third of the hogs that were being marketed were participating in the nickel checkoff program. This raised enough money that the national organization grew and added staff and resources. This happened at the same time that the pork industry was rapidly growing.

I have been involved in ag organizations and groups for nearly fifty years. I have always been a strong believer that, as a farmer, you should help promote the products that you raise and help educate the general public about how food is produced. If I wasn't willing to spend the time, energy, and resources to promote the soybeans, corn, pork, and beef that I was producing, I shouldn't expect someone else to do it for me. I wanted to be involved in making a positive difference on the issues and challenges facing agriculture that would not only help farmers, but also consumers.

There's one thing for sure about farmers; they are good at what they do—producing an abundant supply of high-quality food at an inexpensive price for the consumer, all while caring for the environment. As farmers, we should be proud of the work that we do. Sometimes we do such a good job that we end up with a large supply of a certain product, causing very low prices. By getting involved in these organizations and volunteering my time, I wanted to help other farmers thrive and be successful by expanding their markets, influencing government regulations, and ultimately improving the product for the consumer.

This was a critical time in my farming career and in my personal life. Linda and I had a young family with two daughters. Cindy was born in October 1962, and Lisa was born in June 1966. I wanted to make sure that I was there for my family and was a good husband and father. During this time, I was expanding the farm by increasing the number of sows and the number of acres that I farmed on a regular basis.

My involvement in ag organizations began in earnest in the fall of 1968. Chuck Bloomberg, the executive director of IPPA, ventured to Pike County to help organize a county pork producers association. The IPPA board assigned Chuck the responsibility to increase members and promote the "Nickels for Profit'" campaign. The plan was to establish county groups to be part of the state organization. He worked with Joe Phillips, a well-known purebred Hampshire swine breeder from Pike County; Winfred Dean, a Pike County Farm Bureau leader; and others to help coordinate the initial organizational meeting.

A group of thirty to forty pork producers from Pike County met in the Pittsfield Community Center building in November1968. Chuck gave a presentation about what the state pork association was doing to improve the image of the pork industry, to increase consumption of pork, and to generate a better price for the people producing pigs throughout the country. The group assembled that evening decided to organize into the Pike County Pork Producers Association. They elected me to be the first president of the association. At that time, I was twenty-nine years old. Joe Phillips was elected vice president; Lawrence Smith was secretary, and Winfred Dean was the treasurer.

In the late sixties, Pike County was the second-largest pork-producing county in the United States. Pike County was the self-proclaimed "Pork Capital" of the nation. Henry County, Illinois, was the self-proclaimed "Hog Capital" of the nation. Henry County sold more hogs, but Pike County's hogs were bigger. The two counties had a lot of fun teasing each other over these claims. There was no doubt that pigs were a big part of our county and our economy. As the news spread that I was the president of the county association, I began to get very busy. Pike County Pork Producers organized as a not-for-profit Illinois corporation and held many meetings and had a number of activities. I was also asked to serve on some statewide committees. The Illinois state veterinarian, Dr. Paul Doby, asked me to serve on the state hog cholera eradication committee. I'll discuss that further in the next chapter.

While I was president of the Pike County Pork Producers, we had a pork queen contest. Every county pork association in the state selected a young lady between the ages of eighteen to twenty years old to be its county pork queen. These young ladies went to many activities representing the pork industry. One of the activities was handing out ribbons at the local fair, and another was riding in the different parades held around the county and across the state.

In 1969, a panel of judges selected Laura Baker as the Pike County Pork Queen. Her parents went to the same church as Linda and me, so we were well acquainted, which made it easy for us to work together. Laura was a very active queen who took part in all the activities as well as competing for the state pork queen title. One of the biggest highlights was going to a St. Louis Cardinals baseball game.

The Pike County Pork Producers decided it would be a good promotional idea to give a pig to Red Schoendienst, the manager of the St. Louis Cardinals. I thought he came to Winchester, Illinois, every once in a while, to hunt. I was able to track him down and tell him what we wanted to do.

He was very receptive to the idea and gave me the names of the people in the Cardinals' organization that I needed to work with to make it happen. We could not take a big 225-pound market pig to the ballpark, so we decided to take a small pig, weighing about twenty pounds, and present it to Red. We would then bring the pig back home and finish it to market weight and give it to the charity of his choice.

It was a hot day in July when a group of about one hundred pork producers from Pike County and around the state traveled to Busch Stadium to present the pig at the Cardinal baseball game. Queen Laura and I met some of the Cardinals' staff at the stadium. They took us down under the stadium and into the dugout area where the players were. I am not a big sports fan, so I did not know any of the players or anything about the Cardinals. Laura and I visited with a number of the players and with Red Schoendienst before Laura took the pig and presented it to the Cardinals manager on the pitcher's mound before a crowd of more than forty thousand people.

*Laura Baker, Pike County Pork Queen, presents a pig to St. Louis Cardinals Manager Red Schoendienst at Busch Stadium in July 1969. (Photo courtesy of Lynn T. Spence/*St Louis Post-Dispatch*/Polaris.)*

I was afraid the pig would get loose, and I would end up chasing it around the infield in front of all those fans. Luckily, that did not happen. I believe we stayed in the dugout area until the end of the first or second inning, and then we went back and joined the rest of the people in our group in the stadium.

We found out that we could not take a pig to Missouri and bring it back into Illinois because of the ongoing efforts to eradicate hog cholera. The pig was left in Missouri, and the meat we donated was from another pig raised in Illinois. We later took the meat down to St. Louis and donated it to the nursing home that Red Schoendienst had recommended.

The event proved to be very successful by connecting pork producers to one of the most successful baseball franchises in the country. I had several people ask me, since we lived in Illinois, why we didn't try and do something with the Chicago Cubs. One, we are much closer to St. Louis compared to Chicago and, two, compare the number of World Series championships between the two teams. I think this was one of the first ball game events the pork producers ever had. No doubt the Pike County folks had set the bar high for future events. The promotion received a lot of recognition all across the Midwest and around the country and gave pork and pig farmers some positive media exposure.

More than forty years later, ag groups are still teaming up with sports teams to connect to fans and educate them about agriculture. Many Missouri ag organizations have partnered with the Cardinals recently to promote farmers through the Missouri Farmers Care program. This program is an effort of Missouri's agricultural community to stand together for the men and women who provide the food and jobs on which rural communities depend. The group has been airing ads on the Cardinals Radio Network highlighting farmers and their roles in caring for the land and their animals, as well as showing videos in the stadium during the games. It's rewarding to know that the idea of working with the Cardinals, which the Pike County Pork Producers had many years ago, is still being utilized by ag groups today.

As a side note, Linda is a huge Cardinals fan and makes up for me not being interested in sports. She loves watching Cardinals baseball games on television and follows them closely from spring training through the postseason.

My involvement in the county group would propel me to get further involved at the state level. In 1970 I was elected to represent Pike County and five other counties on the IPPA executive committee. I enjoyed the opportunity to meet more people throughout the state. This broadened not only the number of people that I knew in the pork industry, but also expanded the issues that I was able to work on while representing pork producers.

It's interesting when an opportunity presents itself and gives you a chance to do something that you might not have ever done. In 1971, Curt Perkins was the vice president of IPPA. He decided not to accept the presidency of the organization. A group on the executive committee came to me and asked if I would take the presidency. I was very hesitant at first about this opportunity. I knew it would take a large commitment of my time. I said my uncle Clyde, who I farmed in partnership with at that time, would think it was going to keep me away from the farm too much, and it might jeopardize my future of buying the farm. Winfred Dean, a member of the Pike County Pork Producers executive committee, who played cards with my dad and mother and my aunt Dorothy and uncle Clyde about every month, leaned over and said to me, "Clyde may think that, but he will be very proud of you and will support you." On that afternoon in 1971, in Peoria, Illinois, I was elected president of IPPA.

I can remember very well the first meeting of the executive committee after I was elected president. The ladies' auxiliary organization, called the Porkettes, wanted additional funding, and the state board was very divided on what to do. Mary Jeckel, Russ Jeckel's wife, was president of the Porkettes. Russ and Mary were very passionate about women's programs and the need to have them expanded. I cannot remember what the outcome was or who voted how, but I do remember Russ and Mary being pretty upset about people not supporting the programs. They had both worked so hard to get the voluntary pork checkoff going and to get the organization off the ground. It was difficult for me to be chairing my first meeting when there was such adversity.

The other thing that I remember very well was our discussion about the image of pork producers and farmers. Many people at that time thought of pork producers as dirty, uneducated peasants wearing bib overalls. We had a new and very lively organization, and most people enjoyed what we produced—good pork. To help our image of being professionals, it was decided that the board members would wear suits and ties to all meetings. I would not and did not call on or let any director speak at the meetings if he was not wearing a suit and tie. Many years later, ag organizations are still working on improving the image of farmers.

1971 Illinois Pork Producers Association board of directors. Phil is in the front row, second from left. *(Photo courtesy of Phil Bradshaw.)*

The image of pork producers has changed a great deal over the years. The large investment needed to be in the pig business has falsely created the perception that pork producers are wealthy. However, most producers have had to borrow large amounts money, which makes for a very stressful business.

I recognized that as a leader of the organization, I could have an impact on how others outside the industry viewed pork producers. Many times, I might be the only pork producer that was represented at a meeting, so I always tried to be as professional and courteous as possible.

I was elected to serve as IPPA president a total of three times from

1971 to 1974. Previous presidents and officers had only served two years. This was my intent, and I think the board's plan as well, but when our executive director, Chuck Bloomberg, was selected to be the assistant director of agriculture with the state of Illinois, things changed.

We very quickly started looking for a new executive director. This process went well until some directors got a favorite candidate that they began promoting. The board voted to hire this individual, who did not have any statewide experience, and was not sure he wanted to relocate to Springfield. This was an example where directors needed to be better team players. I felt like it was not the right time to select our new executive director, but the board voted to move forward. They directed me to call the individual and talk with him, but I did not make any firm commitments. Come to find out, before I called him, some other directors had already contacted him and told him he'd been hired. It quickly became apparent that he was not happy in his new job, nor was the board happy with his performance. After a few months, he resigned and left the organization.

This happened at the same time as the election of a new president and slate of officers. Some of the directors came to me and asked if I would serve one more year as president, since we did not have an executive director. I agreed and was elected for a third year. I am the only person to serve three years as president of the Illinois Pork Producers Association. I enjoyed this time very much and hope I did a good job representing pork producers in Illinois.

In 1974, the board hired Larry Graham as the new executive director of IPPA. Many people remember Larry because several years later, he went on to serve as CEO of NPPC for a short period of time.

While I was still president of the board, Fran Callahan, a director from the northeast part of the state, had encouraged us to start a Fighting Illini Pork Club at the University of Illinois. This turned out to be a very good promotional effort. There had been a few small activities held, but nothing major. It took a visit to my dentist to get things really started.

The third weekend of September 1974, an old sow threw a gate up and knocked out my two front teeth. I went to my dentist, Dr. Berry, who was a graduate of the University of Illinois. He suggested to me that we should roast a hog at the University of Illinois football game. I immediately thought of the Fighting Illini Pork Club and how we could use this idea to give the group a greater objective and purpose.

The Pike County Golden Boars was a group formed that would travel and roast hogs for various events. I learned a long time ago that the best way to get people involved in an activity is to publicly acknowledge their participation. The first thing I did was get Dr. Berry; Richard Alspaugh, a prominent businessman in Pike County; Wayne Riley, a well-known farmer in the area; and myself all together and had the local newspaper put a picture and article in the paper telling what we were going to do.

Now Dr. Berry, my dentist, had thought about roasting one pig, but by the time I got through visiting with Fran Callahan, Dyke Edelman from the University of Illinois athletic department, and Bob Blackman, the head football coach at the University of Illinois at the time, we were up to cooking sixteen hogs. We served them in the VIP room, under Memorial football stadium, to the media in the press box at the ball game plus to some of the fans as they entered the stadium.

The Golden Boars cooked hogs for several years at University of Illinois football games and one or two times at Northwestern football games in Chicago. They also roasted pigs at several other events around the Midwest. The Golden Boars went out of existence after about seven or eight years. The Fighting Illini Pork Club disbanded in 2015. It was a good program. I think people enjoyed the activities, and I hope it helped educate the consuming public.

My tenure on the IPPA board expired in 1974. Virgil Rosendale had just been elected on the NPPC board representing Illinois. He went on to serve as president of NPPC. While I was interested in serving on the NPPC board, there was not an opening there for me at that time, and I needed to stay home and tend to my business a little more.

Looking back, my time of being involved in the county and state pork producer groups was very enjoyable. I met many people with whom I will maintain relationships for the rest of my life. I also felt that I had contributed to the organizations at a critical time for the pork industry. My journey of serving in volunteer organizations was just beginning. My experience in the pork organizations would springboard me into many other opportunities in the future.

9 Devastating Disease Leads to Leadership Opportunities

Every occupation has its fair share of trials and tribulations to contend with and work to overcome.

Farmers have many frustrations and difficulties to deal with as part of their career—weather, markets, mechanical breakdowns, pests, weeds, diseases, regulations, and finances, just to name a few. Many of these challenges are out of your control, especially the two big ones—the weather and the markets. The weather, whether it rains or not, has a direct impact on the success of your crop and will also impact the markets and the prices that you receive for your crops.

Many farmers like to complain about the many things that they deal with, especially the weather. It's either rained too much or too little or been too cold or too hot. I once heard a joke that I thought was pretty fitting. What is the difference between a jet airplane and a farmer heading to Florida for vacation? When a plane lands in Florida it quits whining!

I've learned over the years to try to focus on the challenges that I can actually influence and make a positive difference. There's no reason to worry about if it is going to rain or not, because there is nothing that I can do about it.

Farming, like life, is unpredictable and uncertain. It can be easy to become frustrated. Just because you have good equipment, plant the best seed, have very fertile land, and control the weeds, if it doesn't rain, you won't have a crop to sell that year. I've lived through droughts and floods, good years and bad years. That is a constant challenge that can either inspire you to rise to the occasion and work to overcome the odds or buckle under the pressure and throw your hands up in the air and give up. A farmer needs to have faith that the good Lord will provide what you need.

There are plenty of stresses in life, but I've always tried to zero in on the things that I could do something about and then focus my time, efforts, and resources to the task of addressing that particular challenge and improving it.

As I got more involved in ag organizations, I realized that I had an opportunity to target efforts and resources on issues affecting farmers and consumers. These were issues that impacted the livelihood of farmers as well as the well-being of consumers in this country and around the world.

Farmers were pooling their resources financially by paying membership dues to various state and national ag organizations. Also, dollars were being generated by checkoff programs, such as the national hog checkoff that I mentioned in the previous chapter. Checkoff programs were established for many other commodities such as corn, soybeans, and cattle. All of these funds were being utilized to address some of the many challenges that farmers faced. While we may have sat around the board table before a meeting and complained about how little rain that we had received, there was nothing that we could do in the organization to make a difference about the weather. However, there were many issues on which we could have a positive impact.

Working with others to get something done is what excited me and propelled me to get further engaged in organizations. I often used my experiences on the farm to help guide me in deciding where to allocate the collective time, energy, and money of those organizations.

As a livestock farmer, one of the big challenges is dealing with the many diseases that affect your animals. If your animals get sick, it means increased costs for medications and vaccinations and the worst-case scenario is having animals die from the disease, which is lost income. Each species has its own list of diseases you want to prevent or control.

Hog cholera, also known as Classical Swine Fever, is a specific viral disease of pigs. It does not affect any other species. The disease is transmitted easily between pigs, so if one pig on your farm gets infected, more than likely, all the pigs will end up getting the disease. The symptoms can include fever, lack of appetite, diarrhea, paralysis, and for pregnant sows the possibility of aborting pigs. Unfortunately, the mortality rate is high.

Hog cholera was the most devastating swine disease in this country for more than a century. It was first reported in the United States in 1833 in southern Ohio. By 1893, ninety separate areas of infection were known to exist. Outbreaks in 1886, 1887, and 1896 each killed more than 13 percent of the nation's hogs, and more than 10 percent died during the 1913 outbreak. The disease was still costing producers $50 million a year in the early 1960s.[4]

I was able to see the devastation of this disease firsthand. In 1951, my dad and my uncle Walter had several hundred head of hogs that they did not vaccinate for hog cholera. Most farmers vaccinated their hogs for hog cholera starting shortly after World War II.

A pig is vaccinated for hog cholera in the 1950s. (Photo courtesy of USDA ARS.)

It was expensive to vaccinate, so some people chose not to and hoped they would not get hog cholera. Unfortunately for our farm, all the hogs contracted the disease, and all but twelve died.

Research conducted in Iowa in the 1940s showed that the virus remained active throughout the winter in carcasses of cholera-infected hogs buried in the fall, and unburied carcasses of infected pigs remained infectious for eleven weeks during cold weather. This meant that to ensure that the virus did not return and affect another group of pigs on our farm, the carcasses needed to be burned. It was a big undertaking to burn all those dead hogs. I will never forget the sights and smells of that horrific day.

There was some good that came from this devastating event, as this experience helped motivate me later in my life to get involved with livestock disease eradication programs. I wanted to help eliminate diseases that caused hardships to farmers, hurt animals and, in the end, negatively impacted consumers.

As President of the Pike County Pork Producers, I was asked by the Illinois state veterinarian, Dr. Paul Doby, to serve on the state hog cholera eradication committee to help control and eliminate this deadly pig disease. The hog cholera eradication effort was a national program. This gave me some of my first involvement with the USDA in Washington, DC.

In 1961, the eradication of hog cholera was mandated by federal law, and then in 1963 the USDA regulatory officials prohibited the interstate shipment of any pigs that had been vaccinated for the hog cholera virus. This is why we couldn't take the pig to Missouri and then back to Illinois for the Pike County Pork Producers with the St. Louis Cardinals' promotion.

To eliminate a disease of this magnitude took a cooperative effort from many different individuals and groups such as scientists, federal and state regulatory agencies, farmers, organizations, and industry groups. It was because of this collaboration that total eradication of hog cholera was achieved and on January 31, 1978, USDA Secretary of Agriculture Bob Bergland declared the United States hog cholera free in ceremonies in Washington, DC. It had taken seventeen years after the start of the federal-state eradication campaign and 145 years after the first reported outbreak of hog cholera in the United States.

I thoroughly enjoyed my time volunteering on this issue, especially because I felt like I was helping make a difference on real-world challenges facing farmers. I soon realized that there were many other diseases that needed attention and resources, but I was glad to lend my time and talents to help in these efforts.

In 1973, while I was still president of IPPA, my friend Carl Krusa called me and asked what the pork producers' organization was going to do about pseudorabies disease in hogs. Carl had a relatively large outside swine operation in Scott County, Illinois, which is just across the Illinois River from Pike County. I told him that I did not know, but I would find out more information and get back to him. I felt an obligation to help since he was a friend, but also a fellow pork producer dealing with a disease that was affecting his herd.

Pseudorabies (PRV), also known as "Aujeszky's disease" was named after the Hungarian veterinarian Dr. Aladár Aujeszky, who linked the disease in cattle, dogs, and cats in 1902. PRV was not identified as a viral disease in swine until 1909. The disease is caused by the pseudorabies virus in the herpes family. PRV is not related to rabies, but the name was used because the disease may resemble rabies. The disease does not affect humans nor does it affect the meat from the pigs, and the meat is safe for human consumption.

I called the dean of the College of Veterinary Medicine at the University of Illinois, L. Meyer Jones, to learn more about this disease. Dean Jones and his wife actually came to our house and discussed the issue with me. Having access to key people was definitely one of the perks of being the president of the state association. Dean Jones told me that PRV had not been a big issue in swine herds, which was true at that time. He explained that once the disease went through a herd, the pigs would build up immunity, and it would not cause much of a problem. I reported to Carl what Dean Jones had told me, and the IPPA did not do anything at that time related to this disease.

Up until the mid-1970s the disease had not been prevalent in the US swine herd, so there was very little experience in dealing with the disease, and very little was known about how it spread or how to control it. Incidences of the disease began to increase with the widespread introduction of total confinement buildings and continuous farrowing. Additionally, antiserum used in the control of hog cholera prior to this time often contained antibodies to PRV and likely contributed to suppression of clinical signs of PRV on many farms.

The virus can remain hidden in nerves of the pig in a carrier state for long periods of time and then be reactivated. Once introduced into a herd the virus usually remains there, and it can continually affect reproductive performance at varying levels. The virus can survive for up to three weeks outside the pig. Acute outbreaks of disease occur when virulent strains of the virus first infect an unvaccinated susceptible herd.

About a year later, in 1974, the disease surfaced again, this time with Willard Korsmeyer and Vernon Pilenger, who both raised pigs near Beardstown, Illinois. They both had large swine herds, which were mostly housed inside buildings. They had big losses of pigs in their buildings from pseudorabies. At the same time, there had been reports of outbreaks of pseudorabies in Indiana, Iowa, and other parts of Illinois. It was becoming a firestorm that looked like it could quickly spread throughout the country. I did not want to see this disease become such a major problem like hog cholera and wanted to nip this disease in the bud before it gained any more momentum.

I had been attending the Livestock Conservation Institute (LCI) animal health meetings from the time that I had been appointed to the state hog cholera eradication committee. LCI, now known as the National Institute for Animal Agriculture, was the industry organization that was formed to work with suppliers of animals going to the national stockyards. LCI was also the lead organization in the eradication effort for hog cholera. After we had many discussions, it was decided to have a national meeting on pseudorabies to gather information and resources and develop a plan on how to deal with this quickly spreading disease.

We had the first meeting in Peoria, Illinois, in May 1975. A large number of veterinarians and farmers from across the country attended the meeting, as well as state and federal animal health veterinarians. It was decided we needed to investigate the number of outbreaks, how it was being spread, and see what we could do to stop the spread of pseudorabies.

At this time there was no vaccine and no way to control the disease. Fortunately, the disease was only in certain areas and was of low prevalence in those areas. The consensus of those present at the meeting was that pseudorabies should become a reportable disease. This was significant because that meant that farmers would have to begin reporting when their herds were infected to animal health government agencies, which would begin to track where the disease was and where it was moving. It was also agreed to try to limit movement of infected animals to uninfected areas.

A number of companies started working on a vaccine. IPPA helped raise money to develop an antiserum, which turned out to be of little benefit, cost quite a lot of money, and caused many headaches to develop.

Sows from Willard Korsemeyer's farm were taken to a laboratory up near Chicago and were hyperimmunized. Then this serum was given to producers to use on half of the pigs they produced. This is how we determined if it was effective in controlling the disease.

After the meeting in Peoria, a pseudorabies committee was established by LCI, and I was selected to chair the committee. LCI was a well-established nationwide animal health organization, so it only made sense that they be the one to have a committee focused on working on pseudorabies. I can remember very well the controversy and the strong opinions by different leaders in the pork industry regarding the plans to control the disease. Some of the most influential and well-known pork producers wanted to do nothing and hope for a vaccine. Others wanted to control the movement of the infected pigs as much as possible to keep the rest of the animals, the 90-plus percent that did not have pseudorabies from getting it.

I remember Indiana had quite a few cases of pseudorabies, and some of the larger producers and pork leaders did not want to take any actions. Iowa was in the same position because it wanted to develop a vaccine as quickly as possible and not have to control the movement of pigs. Illinois state veterinarian Dr. Paul Doby, who had been one of the leaders in the effort to eradicate hog cholera from the United States, felt we should not let pigs move from farm to farm or to market unless we knew their disease status. To allow pigs to move, we needed to know if they were positive or negative with pseudorabies.

I felt like it was not fair to the majority of the pork producers (more than 90 percent) who did not have the disease, to not protect them. For this reason, I was in favor of controlling the pig movement. I received quite a lot of flak over this decision, but I still think it was the right thing to do. Iowa and Indiana to a lesser degree did not control the movement of their pigs, and they had the highest percentage of infected herds during the eradication.

Discussions had begun within the swine industry about efforts to eradicate the disease. These were not easy discussions as it meant those farms that had pigs infected with the disease would need to be compensated for the animals that were put down. Determining who would make those decisions and where the money would come from were big challenges that we had to overcome.

When Dr. Saul Kit, head of the division of Biochemical Virology at Baylor University's College of Medicine, developed the first gene-deleted herpes vaccine in 1984, the eradication effort changed. Companies had finally developed a vaccine that could be distinguished from the field virus. Prior to that, there was no way to tell the vaccinated animal from a field strain infection. This was a major breakthough for all herpes treatment. *New Yorker* magazine did a full-length article about it and took pictures of my pigs and interviewed Dr. Kit and others, including myself.

At the beginning of the eradication effort, there was no official USDA program for pseudorabies. Several pilot projects were launched in various states including Illinois. In 1985, we established the National Pseudorabies Control Board, which consisted of two representatives from NPPC; two state veterinarians, who were selected by the US Animal Health Association (USAHA); and two representatives of the LCI pseudorabies committee. I represented LCI and was selected to chair the board, which I did for the entire eradication effort. Officially, I still chair the board as we never disbanded.

The duties of the board when first started were to make sure all the states were aware of the many requirements to move pigs from one state to another. Each state had a little different set of requirements, so it was the board's responsibility to make sure that when pigs moved to another state they met all the requirements. Even though the board had no legal jurisdiction, the state veterinarians supported our decisions, which for the most part became the law of the industry.

In 1986, another industry-wide meeting was convened in Peoria to provide an update on all the results from the different pilot projects from various states regarding their eradication efforts. It was agreed that a plan should be developed for a national eradication program. NPPC agreed to put up some funds if the USDA would put up so many dollars to help with the eradication program. Jack Block was the USDA secretary of agriculture and was a livestock farmer from Illinois who raised pigs and knew the pig industry well. He was supportive of the efforts and helped secure funds for the program.

The pseudorabies control board would meet two or sometimes three times a year in person. One meeting was held in the spring at the LCI meeting, and another was held in the fall at the USAHA meeting. Each state would fill out requests for the status of disease control in its state. Then the board would decide if they met requirements for the different stages of the eradication/control program standards, which had been established by the LCI and USAHA. The board served in that capacity until the national pseudorabies eradication program was established in 1989.

While Jack Block was US secretary of agriculture, he appointed me to the advisory committee on swine health protection. The swine advisory committee dealt with many issues, including the feeding of garbage to pigs. At that time, a recently passed law stated garbage had to be treated—basically saying food waste had to be boiled for thirty minutes before it could be fed to pigs. I felt that this was a good thing that would provide more food safety measures. This appointment allowed me to travel to Washington, DC, one or two times a year. I was becoming very familiar with the USDA Animal and Plant Health Inspection Service (APHIS) staff and how things worked in this agency.

The USAHA is the oldest and largest animal health association in the country. It was founded in 1897 to help control livestock diseases in the United States and has more than thirty committees that make recommendations on all animal diseases from zoo animals to buffaloes to pigs and cattle. I had become very active in this organization after having served with LCI as its chairman for a couple of years. In 1984, the allied industry members of the USAHA elected me to the office of third vice president of the organization. At that time, I was the first pork producer to ever hold that position. In 1988 I was elected as president of the organization and was only the third person from Illinois to ever be president of USAHA.

This involvement gave me good exposure to the USDA and the opportunity to work closely on the eradication of pseudorabies. Throughout the 1990s more states were declared free of the disease. In 1989 the Accelerated Pseudorabies Eradication Program began, which involved depopulating infected herds. This program helped reduce the number of infected herds in the United States to just over two hundred. By 2004 all states had been declared pseudorabies free, and PRV was finally eradicated from the domestic swine herd.

This had been a long, hard-fought journey from the phone call from my neighbor in 1973 to total eradication in 2004. Countless hours were spent by me and many others to achieve this goal. I believe these efforts have saved the swine industry millions and millions of dollars over the years by eradicating pseudorabies and having controlled it so that it did not infect all the pigs in the United States.

I am proud to have been involved in working with so many people to eliminate one challenge for pig farmers in this country and to provide a benefit to so many consumers in this country and around the world. In a way, those pigs that died from hog cholera on my dad's farm back in the 1950s helped save the lives of many other pigs.

Foot-and-Mouth Disease Eradication Efforts

Foot-and-mouth disease (FMD), also known as Aftosa, is one of the most contagious and dreaded livestock diseases in the world. The disease is highly contagious and only affects cloven-hoofed animals such as pigs, cows, goats, sheep, and deer. The virus causes a high fever, followed by blisters inside the mouth and on the feet. The blisters cause pain and distress for infected animals and can burst and cause lameness. FMD is usually not fatal, but the disease leads to chronic problems of weight loss and loss of milk production. While the disease negatively impacts the production of meat, it is not a public health or food safety issue.

The disease can easily be spread from one animal to another via contact with other animals and through contact with contaminated equipment, vehicles, clothing, and feed. If one animal on a farm gets the FMD virus, it's highly likely that all the animals will eventually get the disease. Once FMD gets a foothold in an area, it can spread like wildfire from farm to farm. For this reason, there are strict protocols concerning how to contain the disease, which can include quarantines and culling infected animals.

At one time most of the livestock in the world was infected with foot-and-mouth disease. Today most of Europe, all of North America, and most of South America are free of FMD. The United States eradicated the disease in 1929. Many countries around the world are still dealing with

FMD in their livestock herds. Keeping the disease out of the United States is a priority for APHIS, which works tirelessly to protect our country's livestock.

FMD can cause severe implications for farmers, the animal ag industry, and the general economy. FMD outbreaks disrupt livestock production resulting in significant economic losses due to the embargoes by trade partners and the enormous amount of resources used to control the disease. The economic impact of an unchecked FMD outbreak in the United States could reach billions of dollars in the first year.[5]

In 2001 there were a number of FMD outbreaks around the world, including in the United Kingdom (UK). Outbreaks in the United Kingdom were devastating and resulted in more than ten million cows and sheep being destroyed. Tourism in the country virtually came to a standstill to prevent the further spread of the disease. In the end the crisis was estimated to have cost the United Kingdom 8.6 billion pounds, which is the equivalent to $14 billion.[6]

At about the same time as the UK outbreak, South America had an increase in the number of outbreaks occurring across that continent. Since South America has the largest cattle population in the world, the FMD outbreak made this a major worldwide crisis. Most of the media were focused on the UK outbreak with news reports showing piles of infected animal carcasses being burned in order to dispose of them. These images were shown around the world and became a wakeup call to countries, such as the United States, that had eradicated FMD, that an outbreak would be devastating.

The concern that FMD might spread to the United States was very real. The media, both general and agricultural, plus our political and government representatives were focused on the threat from the United Kingdom. Ann Veneman had recently been appointed secretary of agriculture by President George W. Bush. Being a past chairman of the US Secretary of Agriculture Foreign Animal and Poultry Disease Committee and the past president of the US Animal Health Association, I wrote Secretary Veneman a letter pointing out that the biggest threat for an introduction of foot-and-mouth disease to the United States was from South America. Many people traveling from the United States to the United

Kingdom do so for historical purposes, not agricultural. Whereas, many people from the United States and other parts of the world travel to South America for agricultural purposes, including learning about its production practices. This meant that there was a greater risk of people involved in agriculture bringing back FMD from South America rather than the United Kingdom. In addition, the agricultural trade between North and South America continues to increase, which increases the potential exposure to FMD.

The United States has very strict regulations on what animals and animal products, as well as any biological products that might carry a foreign animal or plant disease, can be brought into our country. These procedures have kept FMD out of this country since 1929, which proves the system works. However, no one believes it is 100 percent effective. It's always been my belief that the only way to ensure foot-and-mouth disease is not reintroduced into the United States is to eradicate the disease. The less prevalent the disease is around the world, the less likely it is to be carried into the United States or other disease-free countries.

Secretary Veneman did not respond to my letter for several months, but I didn't take the lack of response as a reason to give up working on this issue. I became well acquainted with Dr. Sebastian Heath while he was working at the Pan-American Health Organization (PAHO). He had taken a new job at the United States Agency for International Development (USAID) and was concerned about the spread of FMD around the world, especially in South America. It was decided that USAID would host a meeting to discuss and evaluate what the United States could do to stop the spread of FMD.

A meeting was held in Washington, DC, in 2003. USAID invited speakers from South America, the United Kingdom, several universities, the USDA, and the PAHO. The meeting was well attended with standing room only. The overwhelming consensus from everyone attending the meeting was that it would be in the best interest of the United States to do whatever we could to help eradicate FMD in South America. Bill Hawkes, the assistant secretary for marketing and regulatory programs at USDA, was one of the speakers. Bill had written me a letter a few days prior to the USAID meeting in reply to my letter to Secretary Veneman. Bill's letter expressed USDA's concern over FMD and offered their support for efforts to help South America eradicate the disease.

It was agreed that the USDA should take the lead on the effort, not USAID. Dr. Jim Butler, deputy undersecretary for the USDA Farm and Foreign Agricultural Services, was asked to put a meeting together to discuss how the Americas could work together to eradicate FMD. PAHO and USDA coordinated and sponsored a meeting for all ministers and secretaries of agriculture from the Americas. The meeting also included animal agricultural leaders and organizations. I worked with Dr. Butler and Dr. Heath to help plan the meeting, which was held in Houston, Texas, on March 4, 2004. Almost every country in the Americas was represented by its minister of agriculture or their designee, and there were representatives from most major animal agricultural groups.

Those attending the meeting decided that a broader and more diversified industry group was needed to support the eradication effort. There were private sector groups already working with the Pan American Foot-and-Mouth Disease Center (PANAFTOSA), a specialized technical center of PAHO. PANAFTOSA was established in the 1950s in Rio de Janeiro to control and eradicate foot-and-mouth disease from the Americas. It had been reasonably successful until the major outbreaks in 2001.

The new group was called the Inter-American Group for the Eradication of Foot-and-Mouth Disease (GIEFA). It was agreed to have one public sector and private sector representative representing each of the PAHO regions of the Americas. The regions were: the southern cone, the Andean area, the Amazon region, Central America, Caribbean, and North America. PANAFTOSA was to be the operational organization, and other organizations were to be consultants and advisers to GIEFA.

Dr. Alfonso Torrres, a former administrator of Veterinary Services for USDA, was appointed to represent the public sector of North America. I was selected to represent the private sector of North America. This was quite an honor for me. At the time I was a member of the board of directors for the Illinois Soybean Checkoff Board, which was strongly committed to supporting its largest user of soybeans—the livestock industry. The board agreed to help with the expenses for me to attend the GIEFA meetings. APHIS had helped with some of my expenses up until this time.

Dr. Torrres was selected to be the president of the GIEFA group. Dr. Torres was from Columbia and received his doctor of veterinary medicine from the University of Nebraska. Because he knew the languages and the culture of South America, he was the ideal first president of GIEFA. I served as president of GIEFA from 2006 to 2009.

Dr. Sebastiao Costa Guedes was selected to be the private sector representative from the southern cone region. Dr. Guedes was president of the Brazilian cattlemen organization. He could speak four or five languages fluently and worked for Bayer in different parts of the world. Dr. Guedes was the driving force behind GIEFA and provided the extra push needed to eradicate foot-and-mouth disease from South America.

Over the years GIEFA had many meetings and traveled to many countries to review their eradication programs. The first meeting I attended was in Bogota, Colombia. I arrived in Bogota at about 10:00 p.m. the day prior to the meeting. Arrangements were made for a USDA employee to pick me up at the airport. He was Colombian and spoke only limited English, and I did not speak Spanish. I remember he was driving a bulletproof van, which was a first for me to ride in this type of vehicle. It seemed as if we drove through the city forever. I had been up late the night before and got up early to catch my flight, so I was very tired. When we got to the hotel, I started walking up the stairs to my room. After only two flights I ran out of breath. I thought I was having a heart attack. As soon as I got in my room on the tenth floor, I lay down and soon felt much better. The next morning, I found out what my problem was. I did not realize Bogota is five thousand feet above sea level, and where the hotel was located was more than six thousand feet above sea level. My body had not acclimated to the thin air at that altitude.

Colombia was a good country to host the GIEFA meeting. Colombia had made great progress in its FMD eradication effort, and the private sector was very involved. The Colombian cattlemen established a cattle checkoff program to raise funds to help with the eradication of FMD. Columbia had a model program that we showed and discussed with many other countries that were having difficulty eradicating FMD. Even though Columbia shares borders with Ecuador and Venezuela, which both had high infection rates of FMD, Columbia's program was so well managed that they had no major FMD outbreaks for many years. It continues to be a good example of what the private and public sectors can do when they work together.

While in South America, Dr. David Ashford, APHIS representative to PANAFTOSA, and I visited with large beef users, such as McDonald's and grocery store chains, to get their support of the eradication effort. Dr. Guedes knew a lot of people and companies in South America and set up a lot of meetings with meat packing companies, grocery stores, and industry leaders for us to visit with about the eradication effort. I think these contacts helped keep key people informed and supportive of the program.

While attending a GIEFA meeting in Santa Cruz, Bolivia, I had a very interesting visit from a man in his midthirties. Bolivia was about to become a socialist government, and he was afraid for his family's safety. He wanted me to help him get his family out of Bolivia before the new government came into control. I felt sorry for him and told him I would see if there was anything that I could do. I spoke to the US embassy, but they told me that they could not start giving US visas to all the people in Bolivia who were concerned about the new government coming into power. The man was at our meeting, and I told him there was nothing that I could do. I never saw this individual again. I have wondered over the years how he and his family fared. The new government did take control of some private property, but I heard of no individuals being injured or harmed under the new leadership.

Bolivia, Ecuador, Paraguay, and Venezuela were the South American countries having the biggest problem with the eradication efforts. Some of these areas were so vast that it was difficult to ensure all the cattle received the FMD vaccine. During a trip to South America in 2006, I went with Dr. Ashford and Ricardo Romero from APHIS to deliver three jeeps that were being given to the Paraguay animal health program to use in the Chaco region.

The Chaco region is a mostly uninhabited, semiarid region where cattle roam free. The region covers portions of eastern Bolivia, western Paraguay, northern Argentina, and a portion of the Brazilian states of Mato Grosso and Mato Grosso do Sul. There had been an outbreak of foot-and-mouth disease in this region where cattle from Brazil, Bolivia, and Paraguay had been exposed to the virus. This caused great concern since the number of outbreaks had declined substantially since 2001. It took two days to drive to where the checkpoints were located on the border between Argentina, Paraguay, and Bolivia.

On the first day, we drove on good, hard-surfaced roads. On the second day, we were in a region where the roads were mostly dirt, and we had to stop to open and close several cattle gates every few miles. We would see a farmstead every once in a while, but nothing else. The interesting thing was that when we arrived at the first checkpoint site, the rancher and his wife spoke English and had been educated in the United States. They wanted me to pick out the lamb they would process and cook for our lunch. I did not know a lot about picking out a lamb to eat, so they helped me. We stayed there most of the day and visited about the problems they encountered vaccinating and monitoring the eradication program at this site where the three countries came together.

Each country thought its outbreaks had come from the other countries. The Paraguay River had changed course over the years, and it was not known exactly where the borderlines were between the countries. Brazil was not far away, so there were also cattle in the Chaco region from Brazil. The Brazilian public and private sectors were very active in stopping the spread of the disease. The one thing that always impressed and surprised me was how well educated and informed the people were, even though they lived miles and miles from any town or other ranches.

My involvement in the FMD efforts would lead me to travel to many countries, including Cuba. In 2008 the chief veterinarian of Cuba invited GIEFA to hold a meeting in Havana at the same time as the Office of International Epizootics (OIE) was having its regional Americas meeting. The OIE is the organization that sets animal health standards worldwide. They developed the requirements and activities that must be accomplished before a country could be declared free of FMD. A country would request a designation of free status from the OIE. OIE would review the information and make recommendations to declare the country status.

The GIEFA group thought it would be good to meet in Cuba, since the Cubans had done a good job keeping FMD out of their country. USDA representatives said they could not attend the meeting due to the governmental restrictions on travel to the communist country. However, they were sure that I could get a permit to travel to the meeting. I wrote to the State Department and asked for the forms and requirements to travel to Cuba. I received the necessary documents and letters and filled those out and returned them quickly. I also called the State Department and asked several questions to guarantee that I was doing everything correctly. There seemed to be no question that I would qualify to attend the meeting in Cuba. I received letters and information about the upcoming trip in the mail but did not get the actual permit needed to travel to Cuba.

Dr. Dorothy Geale, the Canadian public-sector representative to GIEFA, offered for me to travel with them, but it was going to be a good distance out of my way. I made my travel arrangements and would be traveling through Cancun, Mexico, to Cuba. A few days before I was to leave, I called the State Department to check on the status of my travel permit. I was told that I should be receiving the paperwork soon, but no paperwork came. I was scheduled to leave the next morning, so feeling confident that the paperwork would come, I went ahead and flew to Cancun, Mexico. I made arrangements at the hotel for Linda to fax me copies of the papers when she received them. My flight was to leave Cancun for Havana on Sunday afternoon, but I postponed it until the next day, thinking I would get the proper papers from the US State Department.

On Monday I called home, and there were still no papers. I was expected to be in Havana at the meeting on Tuesday, so I decided to go ahead and go to Havana. I purchased a tourist visa, which was a small piece of paper, but there was nothing in my passport saying I was a tourist approved for arrival in Cuba.

I boarded the plane in Cancun, Mexico, and took the short flight to Havana, arriving around lunchtime on Monday. I was pretty nervous about the whole situation. This was the first time that I had traveled anywhere without the proper documents. Because I arrived a day later than I had planned, there wasn't anyone to meet me at the airport, so I was going to have to find my own ride. Two Cuban security officers saw I was nervous and stopped me. I showed them my tourist visa and my passport and told them that I was going to a meeting. That was a big mistake. They did not speak English, and I cannot speak Spanish, so it became very confusing.

They inspected my luggage, removing all of my clothes, and my briefcase, looking through all of my papers.

They detained me for close to two hours. Finally, an older man, who was a security guard, came over and looked at my travel papers. He spoke English, and I told him what I was doing and why I was going to the meeting. He immediately asked the younger security guards to fold my clothes and put them back in the suitcase and to reorganize my papers back in my briefcase. He told me to wait right there, and then he left. He called the Cuban Department of Agriculture minister's office, and in what seemed like only a matter of minutes, there was a car from the department to drive me to my hotel. All the security officers were very nice but very strict. Once they saw I was invited by the Cuban Ministry of Agriculture, they were very supportive and cooperative.

I was not able to call back to the States, but Dr. Geale could use her cell phone and call my home directly. I am not sure why this was the case, but I presume that the United States was blocking all US phone calls from Cuba. Since Dr. Geale's cell phone showed up as a Canadian number, it allowed the call to go through, which allowed me to keep in contact with Linda. I attended the meetings and a few social outings and traveled one afternoon through the Cuban countryside. The Canadians were very helpful in my dilemma of not having the papers from the US government to travel to Cuba. The Cuban exchange rate and fees for US citizens were much higher than for Canadians. When I got ready to pay my hotel bill, it was almost two times what the Canadian bill was. Again, my Canadian friends came to my rescue and put the charges on their bill, and I paid them.

Since the papers never arrived, I decided to travel back home the way I had come, through Cancun, and hope for the best. This was definitely the most stressful trip I ever took. I was sure when I reentered the United States in Dallas that I would be stopped and held by US Customs. I was glad to be part of the trip and to help with the eradication efforts, but it wasn't worth spending time in jail. Fortunately, I did not have any trouble going through customs. It was an experience, to say the least, but to this day I do not know why I did not receive a permit.

The biggest benefit that I felt GIEFA contributed to the eradication effort was from its willingness to visit with both public and private sector representatives. These meetings were often the first time the private sector had the opportunity to visit with the public sector that was running the programs and regulating the industry. The smaller countries appreciated that I listened to their concerns and carried those concerns to PANAFTOSA, USDA, and animal health officials.

Many times, it is difficult for animal health officials and private sector representatives to have an opportunity to meet with the minister of agriculture or other officials that they need to visit with to keep the eradication moving forward. A number of times when I was in Brazil, Dr. Guedes, president of GIEFA, would request a meeting with his friend, and Minister of Agriculture for Brazil, Roberto Rodriguez.

Attending the meetings with me, typically, were: Dr. Albino Belotto, the director of PANAFTOSA; Dr. Jamil Gomes de Souza, the director of animal health for the Brazilian Ministry of Agriculture; Dr. Alan Terrell, USDA area director for Brazil; plus maybe one or two others from the Brazilian Ministry of Agriculture. The meetings were always in Portuguese, even though most in the room could speak English, so Dr. Terrell would help translate for me. We would provide the minister an update on the eradication effort throughout South America and ask for his and the government's assistance in completing the eradication.

One important item that I encouraged Minister Rodriguez to do was to work with Venezuela. Hugo Chavez was the president of Venezuela, and relations with the United States and some other countries were not good. Minister Rodriguez had a conversation with the president of Brazil, Luiz Lula, and urged cooperation between the countries on the FMD efforts. President Lula told me many years later through a translator that he was glad Venezuela made progress on eradication and was glad he could help.

The biggest challenge I had was that all these countries wanted the United States to contribute money to their eradication efforts. The United States didn't have funds allocated to help with eradication in other countries, but the United States did help by having APHIS employees stationed in the impacted countries to help with the eradication effort. We did access some PL-480 funds, dollars allocated for foreign food aid, to help build some livestock facilities and laboratories. These funds are used to provide

US food assistance in response to emergencies and disasters around the world to help improve long-term food security. Most of the members of GIEFA, including me, agreed that money was not the biggest problem facing eradication of FMD. Rather it was the will of the producers and the commitment of the government that was needed to succeed, along with good communications between the private and public sectors.

A number of international groups, plus a number of countries around the world, assisted in the eradication of foot-and-mouth disease from South America. Canada and a number of European countries contributed funds to the Food and Agriculture Organization of the United Nations. The largest part of the expense of the program was paid by the South American public and private sectors. The Brazilian cattlemen were the largest private sector contributors. They made funds available for vaccination in several of the other countries in South America. PAHO was one of the largest public contributors to the eradication. Its funding came from the countries of the Americas.

As I accepted a larger role of leadership on the United States' United Soybean Board (USB), my involvement decreased slightly in the activities of the eradication efforts in South America. Dr. Albino Belotto, director of PANAFTOSA, retired, and Dr. Guedes had some health problems. These two gentlemen had been around since GIEFA began. They had seen the benefits from someone associated with the private sector, like me, visiting the different countries. I believe farmers all around the world feel more comfortable talking and explaining their concerns and problems with other farmers. I was one of the few farmers involved in the eradication efforts and always felt like I could connect with the other farmers, regardless of where they were from. My biggest problem was not knowing the languages. There were always those that would help translate for me or professional translators, but it was difficult to keep in the discussions.

No one can deny the progress the eradication effort has made over the years since GIEFA was started in 2004.

South America had not had a reported FMD outbreak in more than three years until 2017 when Colombia reported two outbreaks of FMD. It was determined that the disease was brought in from Venezuela, which was in a state of complete disarray. Prior to the outbreaks, cattle in Colombia were worth two to three times more than surrounding countries due to them being free of FMD and able to access a larger trade market. This caused more cattle to flow into Colombia from other countries and led to an increased risk of FMD. No one was really surprised when an outbreak finally occurred. Colombia cleaned up the outbreak very quickly.

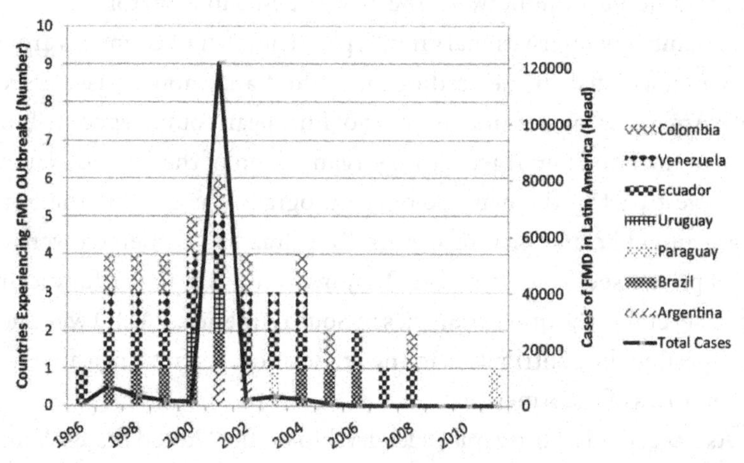

Figure 1 Number of FMD Outbreaks and Corresponding Latin American Countries Where FMD Occurred.
Source: World Animal Health Organization Information Database (WAHID) archives (HandistatusII).

Graph of FMD cases in South America courtesy of Dr. Amanda M. Countryman, associate professor, Department of Agricultural and Resource Economics, Colorado State University[7]

South America is not free of FMD, but the disease has definitely been suppressed with the use of vaccines and animal controls. I believe one of the biggest factors was the fact that livestock producers saw how devastating the outbreaks were in 2001 and knew the only thing to do was to eradicate the disease. The high visibility of the program helped move the eradication effort forward.

Many groups and organizations played a major role in lowering the number of outbreaks across South America. I believe my biggest contribution to the success was showing up at the eradiation meetings and expressing an interest in the eradication effort. South American's successful reduction of infection has lowered the risk of an outbreak of FMD in all the Americas. We must continue to work diligently around the world to eliminate this disease.

11

The Summit of the Americas

I've attended many meetings over the years, but it's not often that I have had the chance to interact with numerous world leaders at the same meeting. In April 2009, I had the opportunity to attend the fifth Summit of the Americas where all the presidents and prime ministers of the Americas gathered to discuss common concerns. Everyone that is except Cuba's President Castro, who was not invited. This caused some hard feelings among certain leaders. The summit was held at Port of Spain in Trinidad and Tobago. There was one day of meetings specifically for folks from the private sector and then two days of meetings for the presidents and prime ministers. The focus of the summit was: "Securing Our Citizens' Future by Promoting Human Prosperity, Energy Security and Environmental Sustainability."

I do not remember exactly how or why I received an invitation. I think it was because I was president of the Inter-American Group for the Eradiation of Foot and Mouth Disease and had worked with many government officials from Central and South America. Whatever the reason, when I received the invitation I decided that this was the chance of a lifetime and decided to attend. It was a good decision.

The first step was to fill out an enormous amount of paperwork to obtain the clearance to attend. They weren't going to let just anyone attend a meeting where all the heads of state from the Western Hemisphere were gathered. The process was very thorough, and I know that someone contacted people I had listed as references. Blair Fortner with the US Soybean Export Council also completed an application and went to the private sector meetings with me.

As you can imagine, the security was extremely tight. The city was blocked off for two blocks all the way around the headquarter hotel—the Hyatt Regency Trinidad. The north side of the hotel was on the waterfront, so it was blocked off to all boats for more than a mile. When we arrived, we were let out of the cab two blocks away. Some people took a bus to the registration area. However, we decided to walk. All of the "low-level" folks like me stayed on a big cruise ship, where the private sector meetings were held. Gunboats, planes, and helicopters from the United States, Trinidad and Tobago, and other countries were constantly patrolling the areas around the hotel and cruise ship.

A number of countries, organizations, and individuals gave presentations on economic development for the Americas. The World Bank, Inter-American Development Bank, regional banks, and others gave presentations on the programs they had to help underdeveloped countries.

Former Illinois Congressman Jerry Weller gave a presentation on what the United States had done and continued to do to help economic development in the Americas. I had known Congressman Weller since he was a boy, as his father, Lavern, served on the Illinois Pork Producers board when I was president in the early 1970s. Jerry had been in leadership of one of the US House of Representatives' subcommittees on Latin and South America. Jerry knew most of the thirty-three presidents and leaders attending the summit.

Jerry and I were invited to attend the opening ceremony with the leaders, which was being held at the Hyatt. When we passed the final security, we entered the lobby of the Hyatt, where the presidents and others were all visiting with another, while waiting to enter the large ballroom. Jerry introduced me to a number of presidents. I shook hands with President Obama but did not visit with him at that time. I met President Obama a total of three times and had the opportunity to visit with him on two of those occasions. I do remember Jerry and I talked to Panamanian President Martin Torrijos for a few minutes about the Panama Canal expansion.

Picture of meeting in Panama discussing Panama Canal expansion. Phil is second from right. (Photo courtesy of Phil Bradshaw.)

As we started lining up to enter the big ballroom for the program, I just happened to walk across the lobby with Secretary of State Hillary Clinton. I remember speaking to her, and she replied by saying something to the effect that she was very tired from a long flight, to which I replied, "You do look tired." If you want to make a good impression on someone, especially a well-known world leader, I wouldn't recommend telling them that they look tired, but that's what came out of my mouth.

Jerry and I entered the big ballroom and found the seats reserved for observers. I remember sitting next to a congressman from New York. The presidents and high-level officials were announced as they entered the room and were seated up front. President Obama and three or four others on the program were seated at the head table. The room had about nine hundred people in it. It was a very entertaining opening ceremony with singing and dancing by the local people.

The president of Argentina, Cristina Fernandez de Kirchner, was one of the speakers and had little good to say about the United States. The following is a portion of her speech as recorded by the Organization of

American States (OAS), which was the official secretariat for the summit. Google Translate was used to translate from Spanish to English.

> At that time (the fourth summit) I think we inaugurated a new way in the sense of planting ourselves in our ideas, in our experiences, and give an answer to what have been doing. Many decades were a traumatic relationship. *First because of Cold War that divided the world and constituted* it into something bipolar. In an East-West conflict that meant for our region hard dictatorships, military interventions, and also paradoxes like for example the expulsion in the year 1962 by the OAS (Organization of America States) of sister Republic of Cuba. Between the arguments for that expulsion was adduced that his (Cuba) adherence to Marxism-Leninism, his (Cuba) accession to the block of the Soviet Union—at that time the other pole of conflict-endangered hemispheric unity and violated the principle of consecrated hemispheric unity by the Inter-American Treaty of Reciprocal Assistance.
>
> I want to tell President Obama of the United States that in no way do I mean a reproach toward him, not at all; he was not responsible for the consensus of Washington or that bipolar world. Nor of injustices that we suffer so many American citizens, on the contrary, maybe he also borders inside his own country. You have felt your civil, economic, or political rights trampled by the color of your skin.
>
> I think we must also account for these transformations, for that suppression of logic of the bipolar world, of the anachronism that means the blockade of sister Republic of Cuba and ask for its uprising (applause).[8]

The president of Nicaragua, Daniel Ortega, also had very negative things to say about the United States. The following is a portion of his speech as recorded by the OAS. Google Translate was used to translate from Spanish to English.

> This summit, which I refuse to call the Summit of Americas ... yes here we are present most presidents, heads of government of Latin America and the Caribbean, are participating the president of the United States, prime minister of Canada, but here are two great absentees one Cuba, whose crime has been to fight for independence, for the sovereignty of peoples; Cuba whose crime has been to provide solidarity, without conditions, to our peoples. That is why he is sanctioned; that is why he is punished; that is why he is excluded; because of that, I do not feel comfortable at this summit, I cannot feel comfortable at this summit! I feel ashamed of me participating in this summit, with the absence of Cuba.
>
> Regarding the US blockade against Cuba and the exclusion of this country from the Summit of the Americas, the countries of the Bolivarian Alternative for the Peoples of Our America, we reiterate the declaration that all the countries of Latin America and the Caribbean adopted last 16 of December 2008, on need to end the economic, commercial, and financial blockade imposed by the government of the United States of America to Cuba including the application of the called Helms-Burton Law, which is widely known.[9]

President Obama just smiled and listened very patiently until it was his turn to speak. Then he handled it very well in his remarks by saying:

> To move forward, we cannot let ourselves be prisoners of past disagreements. I am very grateful that President Ortega—applause—I'm grateful that President Ortega did not blame me for things that happened when I was three months old (laughter). Too often, an opportunity to build a fresh partnership of the Americas has been undermined by stale debates. We've heard all these arguments before these debates that would have us make

> a false choice between rigid, state-run economies or unbridled and unregulated capitalism; between blame for right-wing paramilitaries or left-wing insurgents; between sticking to inflexible policies with regard to Cuba and denying the full human rights that are owed to the Cuban people.
>
> I didn't come here to debate the past—I came here to deal with the future (applause). I believe, as some of our previous speakers have stated, that we must learn from history, but we can't be trapped by it. As neighbors, we have a responsibility to each other and to our citizens. And by working together, we can take important steps forward to advance prosperity and security and liberty. That is the twenty-first century agenda that we come together to enact. That's the new direction that we can pursue.[10]

During the summit, President Obama had accepted the book *Open Veins of Latin America: Five Centuries of the Pillage of a Continent* from the president of Venezuela, Hugo Chavez. The US press was very critical of President Obama for accepting the book. However, I was told by others that it would have caused tension if he had refused to take the book. My only criticism of the president while at the summit would be that he did not acknowledge the programs the United States had helped implement that benefitted the Americas, such as assisting with the FMD eradication efforts.

A number of the presidents and prime ministers used the summit to argue in favor of the United States lifting the embargo on Cuba. President Obama opened diplomatic relations with Cuba in 2015 and moved aggressively to restore economic relations in 2016. This has been good for US agriculture.

I attended all the private-sector meetings held on the cruise ship and the opening ceremony in the general session. These meetings, like most other national and international meetings that I had attended, unfairly blamed many problems on agriculture and food distribution. The summit meeting was like the UN Compact meetings, where there were a lot of very smart people and well-meaning people in attendance, but many of them had hardly any understanding of today's agriculture. I believe that I was the only person at the summit who made a living from farming.

I hope that my involvement in the Summit of the Americas was able to have a positive impact on world leaders and their views on agriculture.

12

Trip to Romania

My favorite movie is *Forrest Gump*. I like to watch how ol' Forrest always winds up in these interesting situations and then finds a way to come out smelling like a rose. It's amazing to me how the writers of the movie were able to tie in so many historical events where Forrest played a role or helped shape the outcome of a historical event.

Sometimes as I look back at my career in agriculture and the many journeys that I have embarked upon, I can relate to Forrest. At the time that all these events were happening around me, I didn't realize the historical significance or the role that I was playing.

Little did I know that a brief meeting between President Clinton and author Salman Rushdie on November 25, 1993, would lead to a treacherous situation during one of my travels. President Clinton had met with the author of *The Satanic Verses,* which had been condemned by the Islamic community as an attack on their religion and which led to a death threat against Rushdie by Ayatollah Ruhollah Khomeini of Iran. The death decree has never been lifted and still remains to this day.

President Clinton's meeting with Rushdie was intended to make a point about free speech and the evils of intolerance and convey America's abhorrence of Iran's refusal to lift the death threat against the novelist. Government officials had warned that the meeting could provoke terrorist or mob actions against US citizens abroad, which included this farm boy from Pike County.

One day in late July 1993, I received a phone call from Cooper Evans, former congressman from Iowa and ag liaison to the White House. I had met Cooper several times during my trips to DC. He had gone back to his farm in Iowa after his years in Congress, and I had always gotten along well with him. Cooper asked me if I'd be interested in traveling to Romania later that year to evaluate a soybean protein supplement program for the private organization Volunteers in Overseas Cooperative Assistance (VOCA), which was partially funded from private sources with the balance from USAID.

There is a rule that requires USAID programs to have a third-party review. USAID asks VOCA to conduct the review using farmer volunteers. Congressman Evans was chairman of the VOCA board, and he knew that I had been involved in various groups. VOCA had sent a team to Romania earlier, but they came home early and did not complete a report.

I agreed to go to Romania. Cooper had said the trip would be interesting, a little dangerous, and include hard living conditions. He was right on all three accounts.

I had to finish harvesting corn and soybeans before I could leave. I left home on November 16 and after two days of briefings in Washington, DC, another farmer from Indiana and I left for Romania. I did not return home until December 23, 1993. This was the longest time that I was ever out of the United States.

Romania was occupied by Soviet troops in 1944 and became a satellite of the USSR in 1948 when it came under communist rule. Nicolae Ceauşescu was the leader of Romania from 1965 until he was overthrown and killed in a revolution on December 25, 1989. Free elections were held in 1990.

The people of Romania had been isolated and under the control of dictators for so long that they had no knowledge of the rest of the world until after Ceauşescu was eliminated. The country had gone from having everything controlled in their society to having no control or regulations on anything. There were no credit cards used, no wire transfers, no checks, and no control over what was sold. All transactions were cash, so when I arrived in Romania I had approximately $8,000 on me.

We were met at the airport by the lady who ran the VOCA office in Bucharest. She and a driver took us to the VOCA office where we put most of our money in their safe. She then drove us over to the Triumph Hotel. This would be my home away from home for most of the time I was in Romania. The hotel was plain but clean and very friendly to all foreign and domestic guests. Once I got my room, I quickly started making friends with the hotel staff. I have found that when traveling alone, it is helpful to develop relationships with those you will be in close contact with. The bell captain and concierge could speak English very well, as could most of the people in Romania.

It was interesting to me that four years after the revolution and overthrow of Ceauşescu, many of the people had no idea about the world outside Romania. It was hard to believe how long and how much the people of Romania had suffered. I met people in their fifties who had never received a permit to go more than one mile from their home. Ceauşescu and his wife ruthlessly ruled the country for twenty-four years. The Romanians with whom I visited thought they were crueler than the Germans or the Soviets. During my travels across Romania, I heard a story repeated many times about one particular farm family that just mysteriously disappeared one night. Grandpa, grandma, mom and dad plus three children were never seen again.

Ceauşescu controlled everything. Dr. Gherman Nicolae was the man who traveled with me as my translator and guide while I was in Romania. He was a good man but had spent his entire life under the rule and dictatorship of the Germans, the Soviets, and Ceauşescu. His wife was a medical doctor, and her job under Ceauşescu was to examine all the babies and decide which ones were not fit for society and then euthanize the babies that were not perfect. The other thing they told me was that Ceauşescu and his wife thought a country needed lots of people to be powerful. I heard on a number of occasions that all women were to have at least two children. If they did not get pregnant, they were forced to be inseminated by another man or artificially inseminated. Abortions were not an option, and if a lady had a miscarriage she would be examined to make sure it was not an abortion. After the revolution there were so many orphans that a number of humanitarian groups came to Romania and set up orphanages.

Due to the money spent on Ceauşescu's extravagant living, Romania was very poor, and the conditions were very hard for Romanians and even those of us who were visiting the country. I remember three young ladies coming into the Triumph Hotel one Friday evening. I could tell by looking at them that they were exhausted and had not had a hot shower in days, if not weeks. I visited with them and found out that they were from the United Kingdom and had been volunteers for two years in a large orphanage not far from Bucharest. The conditions they spoke of in these orphanages were terrible. They hardly had enough food for the children and themselves and had little to no hot water and only enough heat in the buildings to keep the temperature above freezing.

Ceaușescu wanted everything to be grandiose. He thought bigger was better for everything. He built the enormous house where he lived with his wife and bulldozed entire towns and villages out in the country down to nothing and then built large apartment buildings with central heat and water. However, the central heat was of such poor quality that it did not keep the buildings warm. Many families would sleep in the tunnels where the heat pipes ran to keep warm because many of the apartments would be down to below-freezing temperatures in the winter.

I got to experience the cold room temperatures firsthand. The Triumph hotel would keep rooms around forty degrees all the time and seventy degrees from five until seven o'clock in the morning and from five until seven o'clock in the evening. Hotel guests would spend their evenings in the lobby where it was usually warmer. They would gather to watch reruns of the TV show *Dallas*. Since I was one of the few Americans there, people would ask me if that's the way I lived back in the States. I disappointed them because I didn't wear a cowboy hat, wasn't an oil tycoon, and didn't live in a mansion, but I did show them pictures of my family farm.

Large-scale buildings were not the only thing Ceaușescu had worked to create. He also wanted huge farms. The Soviet Union and Ceaușescu took all the land from the people and put it in collective farms. I have visited collective farms in Russia, Romania, and China and have found that they are less productive and unsustainable. There is a lot of good farmland in Romania, but it had been contaminated and almost destroyed by the lack of proper management. Ceaușescu had also built some of the largest livestock confinement buildings, primarily for hogs and chickens, in the world. The buildings were all of poor quality, and the manure system was of such poor design and workmanship that it was a total environmental catastrophe.

After the revolution, farmers both collectively and individually tried to start producing crops and livestock in a more sustainable manner trying to emulate how we do things in the United States. There were a few large pork facilities that I saw where people had attempted to repair and keep these large confinement livestock facilities operating. The Romanians were also trying with their crop farms to transition from the collective farms to individual farms, but no one knew who actually owned the land or who was in control, so it made it very difficult for them to be successful.

The reason the USAID had initiated the soybean protein supplement program for Romania was because they could not produce enough feed for their poultry and pork production. USAID had provided seventeen thousand tons of 42 percent soybean supplement feed. This feed was auctioned off to private farmers at whatever price they could pay. My task was to review the purchases and determine if the soybean protein supplement was used correctly and if the guidelines for the program were followed.

I worked with the International Fertilizer Development Center, which was administering the program in Romania for USAID. I would travel to different farms all over the country and see where the protein supplement was being used, how many animals they had, and how much supplement they had on hand. I visited many different types of farms. Many were big former government-owned complexes now set up as private farm organizations with as many as ninety thousand pigs or two million chickens. I also visited several small private farms with only a few head of pigs, chickens, or cows.

I would discuss with them how they were using the supplement feed. Once they found out that I was a farmer from the United States and had experience in feeding the soybean supplement, they were very receptive and willing to talk. Most were doing a good job of feeding the soy protein supplement along with corn and some milo. The farmers were seeing positive results, with pigs reaching market weight two to three months sooner and chicken broilers weighing 800 grams more at market age.

Several poultry and pig farmers were using less than the recommended amount of soy protein feed because they did not have enough money to buy more. I only found one farmer that had purchased the feed but had no livestock and had no soy protein supplement on hand. I visited with him, and he said shortly after he purchased the soy protein he quit raising pigs and chickens, so he sold his soy supplement to a neighbor. He took me to the neighbor and showed me the soy protein, and both assured me neither one had profited from the sale. He had sold it for the same price that he paid for it, which was not in violation of the program.

After only a few days, the other farmer from Indiana that had traveled to Romania with me decided this experience was not for him. He got on a plane and went home. I would have to say that of the two of us, he was probably a little smarter! I decided to stick it out and complete the task that I had been asked to do. The International Fertilizer Development Center had little Romanian jeeps about the size of our World War II jeeps except that these had a total cab on them. Keep in mind it was late November and early December when I was there, and it was cold. A few days it got down to zero degrees Fahrenheit. Those little jeeps would not get warm—I think because they did not have thermostats in the radiator. I suggested that we cover part of the radiator to contain the heat of the engine. All the drivers said they could not do that because it would not be approved by their supervisors. This unwillingness to make decisions on their own came from years of being controlled and told what to do.

One day when the drivers in the two jeeps that we had with us went inside to get warm and have a smoke, I got two paper sacks that the soy protein had been shipped in and put them behind the grill and in front of the radiator. They did not see me do this, so I felt safe. We started back to our hotel, and I noticed the driver and my translator/guide had put their hands down to the heater where it was starting to get warm. The next day I noticed the other two jeeps had paper sacks in front of their radiators!

Having access to quality gas for our vehicles was an issue in the rural areas. Since there were no government regulations or inspections, you did not know if you were purchasing watered-down gasoline or kerosene. There was also no guarantee that there would be gas available to purchase. This meant that we always carried gas with us. Some of the jeeps carried gas in cans on the back, but oftentimes I rode in the back seat with a twenty-five liter can of gas on both sides of me. Gherman would also have a twenty-five liter can under his feet in the front seat. You definitely didn't want to light a match inside the jeep because we would have gone up in a ball of flames.

The first night out in the field we went to a farm east and south of Bucharest down close to the Danube River and Constanta. The weather was bad that day with freezing rain and a little snow making the roads very treacherous. We passed a young lady carrying something small. I asked if she was carrying a baby, and they said yes. I then asked why she was walking in such bad weather with no gloves on her hands, only a small light jacket, nothing on her head, and only a blanket over the baby. She was several miles from any town or any houses. I was told she had gone to the hospital to have the baby and was walking home. I said, "Let's give her a ride," but the translator/guide said no. I then proceeded to say very clearly that this Jeep belonged to the United States of America, and we were not leaving the young lady with a new baby walking in the snow and ice. We went back and picked her up. I know she had frostbite. We took her directly to her home. No one said a word, but the driver smiled. He was very pleased that we had done this.

That night we had reservations at a hotel in a small town. There was one room for the guide and the driver and one room for me. When I got in my room, I realized there was no heat in the hotel. I also had no running water, but instead had a bucket that they would bring water in to flush the toilet. The front desk staff brought a bucket of hot water for me to wash and shave in, and then I used that to flush the toilet. I slept in all my clothes to try to stay warm. I was reminded that in preparing for the trip, the staff at VOCA had told me to wear insulated boots and insulated coveralls while I was over there, because it would be cold. They were right. The next morning when I got up it was only ten degrees Fahrenheit in my room!

While checking out, I was told that the room only cost $11.50 for the night. When we got in the Jeep and started down the road, I asked Gherman if next time we could have a room with running water and a little heat to keep it above freezing. He said that he could get me a better room, but they couldn't afford to pay for a nicer room. I remembered the nearly $8,000 that USAID/VOCA had given me for expenses. I knew this was more than I would use, so I told them I would pay for their room at a better hotel. They were very appreciative.

I had been in Romania for a couple of weeks when I had one of the most frightening things happen that I have ever experienced in my travels. I had gotten back to the Triumph hotel from being out on farms all week. I was dirty and rough-looking, so I went to my room and cleaned up while it was still 70 degrees. It was about eight o'clock when I went to the hotel restaurant to have my supper. There were very few people in the restaurant. By this point all the hotel staff knew me, and I felt very comfortable and relaxed. I ordered my usual and was joking with the waiter a little. When she left to go to the kitchen, a very strong-looking, partially bearded man approached me on my left side and another man came up on my right. The man on my left spoke English. I'm not sure how much English the man on my right side knew, but he could repeat what the man on my left said. They both were in their thirties and looked like they were up to no good. The man on the left said, "Why do you Americans think you can run the world?" I responded rather flippantly that we can't, and it was a good thing that we can't. I was getting an uneasy feeling about the situation. He then said, "Why don't you go home, Yankee? Romanians do not want you over here." Then they both started yelling very loudly at me, "Yankee, go home" several times.

By this time, I realized that I was in trouble. I tried to remain calm because I sure didn't want to escalate the situation any further. I just laid my hands on the table and said nothing, not knowing what was going on or why. I had visions of them slitting my throat right there; they just looked like hoodlums. Then a little short lady who looked to be around sixty years old came to the door of the lobby and yelled something in a foreign language to warn the two men. As quick as they had appeared, they disappeared by darting through the lobby and out the front door. As they ran out, Romanian police with automatic weapons came in the side doors from the kitchen to the lobby. There must have been eight or ten of them with their automatic weapons ready to use. This looked like a scene from a movie, but it was real. I do not know to this day if they ever caught the two men or the lady.

It didn't take me long to figure out why they had been yelling at me. I had been out in the field and had not opened the message from the embassy warning me to be on high alert for possible attacks on Americans.

The Iranian government had told their people to harass Americans because President Clinton had met with Rushdie.

Everyone in the hotel was a little afraid of what was going to happen. The police said little to me, and they went after the two men and the lady. It seemed I was the only one in the hotel who did not realize that they were Iranians and not Romanians. The hotel gave me my dinner at no charge, and I enjoyed it, but I was a little bit nervous the rest of the evening. There were a number of Iranians in the hotel who I had visited with on different occasions. I remember one gentleman from Iran who was an electric motor salesman. He was very nice and spoke almost perfect English. He came up to me later in the evening and apologized for this behavior.

Aside from the dangerous situation and uncomfortable living conditions, I was glad I had traveled to Romania and helped with the program. It was a valuable program that was doing good work. The money the Romanian farmers paid for the soybean protein supplement was partially used to fund a program designed to help Romanians reclaim ownership of their land after fifty-two years of government control.

The trip reminded me of what Forrest Gump had said: "Life is like a box of chocolates. You never know what you're gonna get." I have found that to be true of many of my adventures but especially this memorable trip.

Checkoff Programs Benefit Farmers and Consumers

If you enjoy eating shrimp, whether at home or in a restaurant, you can thank an Illinois soybean farmer. It may seem odd to connect seafood with a Midwest soybean farmer, but raising shrimp is one of the best examples of a farmer-funded checkoff program benefiting consumers.

Checkoff programs help farmers expand their market share and increase their revenue by promoting their products to consumers. The products that are produced from our farm are corn, soybeans, and pigs.

The corn and soybeans that we grow, along with thousands of other farms in this country, are ingredients in many products that consumers use every day. The majority of corn grown in the United States is field corn. This is not the same as vegetable corn that you eat as corn on the cob or corn in a can. The corn from our farm might end up in your bowl of corn flakes or bag of corn chips or be made into ethanol to fuel your vehicle.

My corn and soybeans aren't much different than my neighbor's crops down the road, although we may use different methods to produce these products. For example, I use Massey Ferguson tractors; my neighbor uses John Deere. I plant Pioneer seed; my neighbor plants DeKalb. After harvest, when farmers haul their crops to the grain elevator, the corn will get mixed together, and you are unable to tell which corn came from my farm and which corn came from my neighbors'. The same is true for soybeans.

We call the corn and soybeans we raise a commodity because they are products that meet similar standards for quality and safety. It is difficult to differentiate commodities, and thus the price that farmers receive for their commodities is the same.

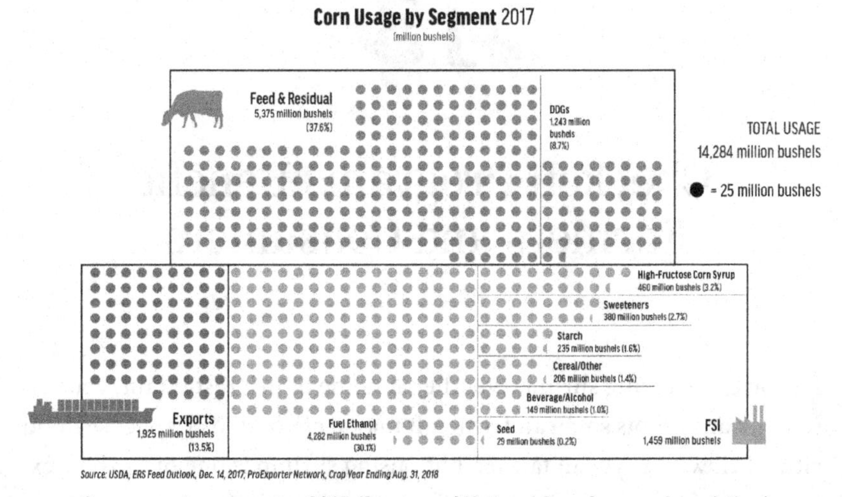

Corn usage by segment—2017 (Courtesy of National Corn Growers Association.)

This is very different than many industries that work hard to differentiate themselves and their products from their competitors. The objective of increasing commodity markets takes cooperation between individual farms and businesses. I have always found it interesting that farmers can be competitors when bidding on a piece of land at an auction or trying to rent a piece of ground but also work together through a checkoff program that promotes their commodities.

Consumers may not know exactly which farm raises their corn, soybeans, or pork, but they will decide what to buy based on knowledge, quality, and availability. The consumer's understanding that there is a general uniformity to commodities serves as the reason for individual farms and businesses to work together on a comprehensive, industry-wide strategy to expand their markets. Promoting a commodity, such as soybeans, rather than a specific company that processes soybeans, means everyone in the industry benefits. Checkoff programs are designed to help increase sales and consumer awareness and create higher overall demand for a specific commodity.

Checkoff programs allow farmers to pool resources for advertising campaigns, market research, new product development, and consumer education. They are completely funded and operated by industry stakeholders. There are currently twenty different national checkoff programs in the United States representing a wide variety of commodities.

Commodities by Annual Checkoff Revenue
(includes money collected at the federal level; some checkoffs have an equal amount of checkoff returned to the state level)
Source: USDA Agricultural Marketing Service

Commodities by Annual Checkoff Revenue - 2016

Commodity	Checkoff Revenue
Dairy	$332.1M
Fluid Milk	$94.8M
Soybeans	$89.5M
Cotton	$74.1M
Pork	$70.3M
Hass Avocados	$54.7M
Beef	$39.1M
Paper & Packaging	$24.3M
Eggs	$23.6M
Potatoes	$14.0M
Softwood Lumber	$13.2M
Peanuts	$9.6M
Sorghum	$9.4M
Blueberries	$7.9M
Mangoes	$7.4M
Honey	$6.7M
Mushrooms	$5.0M
Watermelons	$3.5M
Lamb	$2.4M
Christmas Trees	$1.7M
Raspberries	$1.6M
Popcorn	$0.6M
Total	$885.5M

Many of the commodity checkoff programs started in the late sixties or early seventies.

The pork producer voluntary pilot checkoff that was started in 1968 has been successful. At the same time that the pork producers were working on their voluntary program, the soybean farmers in Illinois and around the nation were also looking at starting a checkoff program. The proposal was for up to one half cent per bushel to be deducted from the soybean farmer's check at the first point of sale. The soybean checkoff was taking a little different approach in its efforts, which were being driven by the American Soybean Association (ASA). The idea was to pass legislation within each state to allow a referendum asking soybean farmers if they would be in favor of starting a soybean checkoff.

The legislation passed in Illinois, and a referendum was held. Farmers approved the program, and the soybean checkoff has been funded ever since. The legislation allowed for periodic referendums to ask farmers if they approved raising the checkoff rate. The Illinois soybean checkoff started at one quarter cent per bushel and was raised to one cent per bushel before the national checkoff program was established.

Several states passed soybean checkoff programs, but many did not. It was unfair to producers in the states with a checkoff to be funding soy promotion, research, and other activities while producers in other states were paying nothing but were still reaping the benefits. This led to the discussion for the need to start a national checkoff program where all farmers would pay into the program.

There were some larger-producing soybean states, like Indiana, that did not have a checkoff program. Representatives from Illinois and other states visited with farmers, marketing representatives, and political leaders in Indiana to convince them to start a state checkoff. However, farmers in Indiana were not ready to support it. In the late 1980s and early 1990s, commodity groups started promoting and working for national legislative checkoff programs. The only commodity group that I know of that did not pass a national program was the corn growers.

Each commodity group has a different approach to how their checkoff is handled and administered. How to govern the commodity organizations was one of the big challenges as commodity checkoff programs were started. Some checkoff programs are state programs supervised by the state, while other commodity programs are national and are under the direct supervision of the USDA secretary of agriculture. For example, soybeans, pork, and beef are national checkoff programs while corn is a state checkoff program, which was established in 1982. The Illinois Corn Marketing Board collects and administers the 5/8ths of a cent checkoff on each bushel of corn sold.

Research has proven that checkoff programs are a good investment for the farmers that contribute to them. According to the results of the soybean checkoff's most recent independent return-on-investment analysis, all US soybean farmers receive $5.20 in profits for every dollar they invest in the checkoff.[11]

You will probably recognize several of the advertising taglines that were developed by checkoff programs such as: "Got Milk?"; "Pork. The Other White Meat"; and "Beef. It's What's for Dinner." Since the dairy industry's "Got Milk?" campaign was launched in 1993, it has become a part of popular culture by generating many funny spinoffs featured in TV shows and ads. The campaign exceeded its original advertising plan with the "Got Milk?" message displayed on more than seventy-five products, such as toys, posters, and clothing. The campaign has successfully garnered the support of a new generation of milk consumers.

While the checkoff programs are great for the farmer, there are actually many benefits to the consumer as well. Checkoff-funded research has helped improve production practices, which helps lower the cost that consumers pay for products. As I mentioned in the beginning of the chapter, consumers wouldn't be able to purchase shrimp at an affordable price had it not been for soybean farmers investing checkoff dollars to determine how to raise shrimp in captivity.

The number of shrimp the world was consuming was fast depleting the wild shrimp population. The soybean farmers in Illinois and throughout the nation invested $3 million to $4 million in research and educational efforts to develop the breeding and the feeding of shrimp in captivity. We worked with Texas A&M University on the project. This effort made it possible for most consumers worldwide to continue to have shrimp available at a price they could afford, while also increasing demand for soybeans.

As Bubba told Forrest Gump, "Shrimp is the fruit of the sea and can be fixed a variety of ways." Shrimp is the most consumed seafood in the United States, according to the National Fisheries Institute. Americans ate more than four pounds of shrimp per person in 2011. I know farmers who converted old hog barns into buildings now used to raise shrimp. More than 90 percent of the shrimp eaten in the United States is farmed overseas. In fact, shrimp makes up more than 30 percent by value of all seafood we import. We mainly import shrimp from Southeast Asian countries such as Thailand, Indonesia, and China, followed by Ecuador and Mexico.[12]

Another recent program funded by the soybean farmer is deep water fish cages. Large cages of fish are placed out in the ocean and are designed to go deeper as the sea gets rougher. The fish are fed a soybean-based feed and are easy to harvest, making for a very inexpensive seafood for a hungry world population.

Consumers have also benefitted from checkoffs through improvements to the environment and improved products. For example, the Cotton Board began its "Cotton. From Blue to Green"® program in 2006 by partnering with an insulation manufacturer to convert used jeans into denim insulation. Instead of the used jeans going to a landfill, they are being used for a different product that is environmentally friendly. The program promotes cotton through a less traditional use of its product, while creating opportunities for community partnerships with the likes of Habitat for Humanity.

Take the "Pork. The Other White Meat" campaign as another example. The campaign has helped educate consumers that pork is a lean and healthy protein choice. Efforts to develop new recipes and ways to prepare pork were funded with pork checkoff dollars, as were efforts to educate farmers on improved production and feeding practices that lowered the fat content of the pork, producing a healthier product.

Pigs on our farm usually go to the JBS processing plant in Beardstown, Illinois, or the Farmland plant in Monmouth, Illinois. The pork checkoff doesn't promote just JBS or Farmland pork, but rather promotes commodity pork in general to consumers. As consumers feel good about eating pork, they purchase more pork, and the demand for pork goes up, and that results in higher prices for my pigs.

Getting a diverse group of producers to join together and develop integrated messages and campaigns is another benefit of checkoffs. A good example of this is the National Mango Board. Before this checkoff began, the mango industry was disjointed, and producers competed against each other with no vision for the future and little success in growing their markets. The checkoff program provided a means for those involved in mango production to share knowledge and ideas and develop a campaign with unified messages. Consumers were educated on the nutritional value of mangos and were motivated to try new recipes, which led to market growth. Consumers now eat nearly six pounds of mangos per person annually compared to just two pounds in 2008 when the board was first launched.[13]

Checkoff programs have expanded and created identities for things we use every day, increasing consumer awareness and expanding markets for many US commodities.

The bottom line is that if farmers didn't have the checkoff programs, there wouldn't be anyone telling our story, promoting our products, looking for new uses, and inventing new production techniques.

The Soybean Checkoff

In the early 1980s, I was purchasing soybean meal every three weeks from Quincy Soybean in Quincy, Illinois. I used the soybean meal to mix with ground corn to feed my pigs. This amounted to about seven tons of soybean meal that my farm was consuming every week, or more than 360 tons on a yearly basis. The soybean checkoff was promoting new uses of soybeans, such as soy crayons and soy candles. I thought the checkoff needed to be spending more time and funds promoting the largest consumer of soybeans—livestock!

Rather than just calling the soybean office to complain, I decided to get involved and do something about it. I believe if more people in this country took this approach, we would have fewer problems, but let's be realistic; it's much easier to complain than to take action and get something done.

In 1984 there was an opening on the Illinois Soybean Checkoff Program Operating Board, also known as the Illinois Soybean Checkoff Board. This board administered and had oversight of the state soybean checkoff funds. I needed 250 soybean farmers to sign a petition for me to be on the ballot to represent seven counties in west central Illinois. I was able to get the 250 signatures, and in the election, I received a few more votes than a man from Greene County and was elected to the board.

There were two separate boards at the state level. The Illinois Soybean Checkoff Board dealt with checkoff programs, and the Illinois Soybean

Association board dealt with the political and governmental affairs. There were eighteen members on each board, representing districts across the state of Illinois.

The board of directors of the Illinois Soybean Association in 1984. Phil is pictured in the second row, second from left. *(Photo courtesy of Phil Bradshaw.)*

One of the first things I did was encourage the Illinois Soybean Checkoff Board to contribute money to the US Meat Export Federation (USMEF). The board chose to contribute and was given a director position on the USMEF board, which I was selected to hold. That is when I first started attending USMEF meetings. Although I was never in a leadership position with USMEF, I did serve on the executive board on two occasions. I also traveled to Venezuela, the island of Curacao, and Mexico with USMEF. On these trips we educated local hotel chefs and meat importers about how US meat could be prepared and explained to them where and how they could purchase and ship it to their location. We wouldn't now be exporting 26 percent of our total pork production, worth nearly $6.5 billion, to foreign destinations[14] if it hadn't been for the USMEF receiving soybean checkoff dollars making it possible to reach out and touch those markets.

Facts on US Pork Exports[15]

- From 2008 to 2018, the United States, on average, has been the top exporter of pork in the world; it is the globe's lowest-cost producer of pork.
- Exports have added $53.47 to the average price, or a total of $147 that producers have received for each hog marketed in 2017.
- Pork exports help support an estimated 550,000 mostly rural jobs, including 110,000 jobs tied directly to exports.
- Based on export success and unprecedented demand for its product, the US pork industry is currently on pace to expand production over the next two years by 8 percent.

The General Agreement on Tariffs and Trade (GATT) went into effect after World War II to lower tariffs and increase trade throughout the world. In 1987 the United States won a GATT case concerning the export of vegetable oil to European countries. The US complaint claimed that European countries were giving subsidies to companies for processing European-grown soybeans. I was chairman of the Illinois Soybean Checkoff Board and decided to lead a group to Germany to visit with them about the trade of soybean oil and how to work out our differences. The board agreed to pay my way, and I paid for Linda to go too. We asked other soybean farmers to go, if they wanted to pay their own way. We hosted a dinner and meeting at the US embassy in Bonn, Germany, for those who were involved in the importing of soybean oil and those involved in the industries that the United States was allowed to put tariffs on to offset the tariffs on our soybean oil. It was a very nice setting overlooking the Rhine River. After our meetings in Germany were done, we took an electric train from Munich, Germany, to Venice, Italy. It was the same route the Orient Express took, and our train was very similar to the one in the movie *Murder on the Orient Express*. It was a beautiful trip through Austria and the Alps.

In Venice we meet with Italian officials and a family who ran a restaurant and a vegetable oil processing business. A few years earlier the ASA, using soybean checkoff and USDA matching dollars, introduced this family to new uses for soybean oil and helped them expand their business. They increased their business tenfold, so they were very interested in meeting with us. Next, we took the train from Venice to Geneva, Switzerland, to the UN headquarters. We visited with UN officials about world trade and the soybean oil trade issues with European countries. The differences were worked out over time. I do not know how much our meetings helped, but our soybean and oil exports have grown over the years.

Soybean farmers are always looking for new markets for our soybeans. I have been on many trips with the purpose of trying to open up a country's market for US soybeans. It's simple economics—the more soybeans that we can export around the world, the greater demand for soybeans, which leads to higher prices for soybeans. Sometimes you forget that you are growing a commodity that can help improve the health and lives of people less fortunate.

Top Destinations for US Soybean Exports *(3-year average through 2016/17; tonnes)* *Data Source: U.S. Census Bureau*	
China	32,065,704
EU-28	4,947,269
Mexico	3,680,826
Japan	2,309,803
Indonesia	2,237,804
Netherlands	1,734,664
Germany	1,568,034
Taiwan	1,457,143
Spain	950,251

In 2000, US soybean farmers from state soybean grower organizations, including the Illinois Soybean Association, created the World Initiative for Soy in Human Health (WISHH) as a program of the ASA.

The program's objective is to help provide soy protein to poor people around the world. Since its inception, WISHH has been enhancing the protein intake of many nations through market development, education, and research.

ASA set up a committee to work with state soybean groups and farmers in carrying out the program. WISHH was seen by some farmers as more of a charitable effort than a market expansion program, but in reality, it is both. As we improve the lives of lower-income people in developing nations, they will improve their diets and become tomorrow's customers for US soy and soy protein.

Since it has a humanitarian component and is not solely a market expansion effort, ASA has continued to manage the WISHH program. USB has provided some checkoff dollars as grants for specific programs, but most funds came from other sources. State Soybean Associations are one of the major funding sources, along with individuals, companies, foundations, and others.

Jim Hershey is the executive director of the WISHH committee and works with many groups and organizations to identify low-income countries that are protein deficient in their diets and could benefit from soy protein being added to their diets. This program has grown to where activities are carried out in several countries around the world including Africa, Asia, and Central and Latin America. Most of these countries' programs are for children or for HIV/AIDS patients who need high levels of protein in their diets to help the medicine control the disease.

I was fortunate to serve as chairman of the WISHH committee and visited several countries including Honduras, Vietnam, and Ghana. In Honduras, we worked primarily with school children. The first lady of Honduras was very helpful and supportive of our efforts to improve children's diets. The program was very simple. We would have a human nutritionist look at what children were eating and estimate the protein they were receiving. Then the mothers and school staff would add enough soy protein to their food so each child would have the protein he or she needed for a healthy life. I had the opportunity to see children before and after they received adequate protein. In a lot of the children it was easy to see the difference in their health. Their skin color was better, their hair was much brighter, and they looked healthier overall.

In Vietnam we focused much more on HIV/AIDS patients. The Vietnamese government isolated people who were positive with the HIV virus. While we were there, they were treating patients with good medicine but did not have good protein sources. By adding soy flour to their diets, the medicine was more effective.

One evening we took a tour of the famous Hanoi Hilton. We saw where Senator John McCain and other US servicemen were chained for years as prisoners during the Vietnam War. The Vietnamese people that I met had positive feelings toward Americans but not of the US government due to tensions from the war. One of the ladies, who was using US soybeans to make a soy jam, welcomed us to her business but said to us through a translator that the US government had killed one of her sons during the war. It was good to be a part of the WISHH program that was attempting to help so many people that had already suffered so much.

In Ghana we visited with both public and private sectors about their need for more protein. We saw a fish production trial that they were running and also looked at a very modern feed mill that a group from Israel was building. The principal purpose of the visit to Ghana was for us to show them how to increase the protein in their diet. The government officials were very eager to visit with us about how to increase their soybean production and how to import more soybeans for livestock and human use.

My involvement in the WISHH program has reminded me how fortunate we are in this country and is an example of positive things being accomplished when we work together. It also solidified my strong belief that we must use every means necessary to continue to feed a growing world population. The number of mouths that need to be fed will continue to increase, and the only way that we will be able to feed everyone is with innovative technology and techniques that continue to increase our production.

One of those technologies that we, and many other farmers, have used is genetically modified organisms (GMOs). The name, genetically modified organisms, has led to many misperceptions by consumers in this country and around the world. Europe and countries around the world were rejecting GMO crops from the United States, including soybeans. In 2006 the USB board decided a trip to Europe to discuss GMOs with both the public and private sectors was needed to find out what we could do to help open this very important market to our GMO soybeans.

David Green of Greenhouse Communications was asked to put a trip together. David was originally from Ireland and was very well acquainted with both the public and private sectors in Europe. The trip was well planned and organized, and we participated in numerous meetings with industry and government officials in three European Union (EU) countries—England, Belgium, and Germany.

While in London, England, we stopped and visited with Nestlé's and other food companies, plus members of the parliament. Kim Nill with US Soybean Export Council (USSEC) brought many copies of documents on GMOs and US regulations covering GMOs with us to Europe. We gave this information to everyone we met and asked them to reconsider their position on importing GMOs. The EU requires mandatory traceability and labeling of GMOs, which have disrupted the soybean trade with the United States and decreased the availability of soybean-based products in the EU.

We traveled from London to Brussels, Belgium, where we met with USDA officials and visited with members of the European parliament concerning increasing the acceptance of GMO soybeans in the EU.

We had planned to go to Hamburg, Germany, but had an incident while we were at the Brussels Airport that prevented us from going. An individual had pushed past the security checkpoint and was in the boarding area. Security officers were searching for the person, but they could not find him, so the airport was locked down. We were in the airport most of the day and missed our flight to Hamburg, so we went straight to Berlin, Germany, without our bags.

In Berlin, we were met by Bill Westman, US ag counselor general. I had known Bill from his long tenure of working in Brazil and China. Bill provided us with a lot of background information about ag trade. He also set up meetings with German officials where we discussed the importation of GMO soybeans.

It was very apparent during the trip that the American soybean industry is well respected. Even those individuals who had strong opposing views were very interested in the information that we provided them. Most of the people we met with were supportive of GMO crops. It was interesting to me that no one ever questioned the safety of the GMO food. Any concerns were about the perception, sustainability, and environment. The trip proved that we need to keep telling our story and sharing positive information on GMO crops and products produced from GMO soybeans every chance that we get. I believe that farmers and agricultural industries need to learn from the GMO experience and in the future need to make every effort to educate the general public about new technologies before putting a new product on the market.

Another interesting soybean trip that I went on was a trip to Russia in 2008. Russia had not been a large user of soybeans from the United States but imported a lot of soybeans and soy products from other countries. USSEC decided it would be good for farmers to go and visit with those individuals responsible for importing soy. This turned out to be an exciting trip for me personally.

My personal medical doctor thought it would be a good idea if I had a health checkup before I went on the trip. My older brother had recently had some heart problems and had open-heart surgery. I had a heart stress test ten days before I left for Russia and received the doctor's approval to travel. Upon entering Russia through St. Petersburg and clearing customs and immigrations, suddenly, two young Russian soldiers grabbed me by both arms and dragged me away. It all happened so fast that no one in our party saw them take me into a small room.

They could speak very little English, and I could not speak Russian. They knew the word *heart* and asked about my heart, but I did not understand and did not think of the stress test I had taken. The lady who represented USSEC in Russia was looking for me by this time. It seemed like a long time, but she found me, along with a Russian official who spoke English. Come to find out, the stress test I had taken left a nuclear dye in my blood, and the Russian test equipment in customs had picked up traces of it, even ten days after I had the test. They gave me documentation to show to officials if I were to get stopped again. Our translator said the documents read like I was a container of hazardous materials.

I got stopped two more times while in Russia. One time was when I entered the Kremlin in Moscow, and the other time was in Kaliningrad, a small track of land Russia has between Poland and Lithuania on the Baltic Sea. Kaliningrad is a political and geographic anomaly since the region is separated from Russia and is surrounded by North Atlantic Treaty Organization (NATO) member states, Poland, and Lithuania. It's closer to Berlin and Prague than it is to Moscow and St Petersburg. Since Kaliningrad is located on the Baltic Sea, this is where many of the soybeans and soy products enter Russia. We had a lot of good discussions about trade and problems with doing business together, but I think both the Russians and our trade team knew the problems were above our authority and would take years to resolve.

One of the by-products of soybeans is soybean oil, which can be used as a vegetable oil in such things as cooking oils. Soybean oil can also be used to make biodiesel, which is a renewable, clean-burning diesel replacement that reduces our dependence on foreign oil, creates jobs, and improves the environment. The Environmental Protection Agency (EPA) has recognized the value of biodiesel by designating it as the first and only advanced biofuel in commercial-scale production across the country and the first to reach one billion gallons of annual production. The other good thing about biodiesel is that it can be used in blends of 5 to 20 percent in existing diesel engines without modification and is covered by all major engine manufacturers' warranties.

Biodiesel is a success story of the soybean checkoff, which helped develop and grow the biodiesel industry by funding research and promotion efforts to ensure that biodiesel remains one of the most tested and used renewable fuels on the market. Demand for biodiesel increases the demand and the value of US soybean oil by eleven cents per pound, adding sixty-three cents of value to every bushel of soybeans.

US consumers used a record of nearly 2.9 billion gallons of biodiesel and renewable diesel in 2016, almost a 40 percent increase from the previous year. Domestic demand for biodiesel accounts for more than a quarter of all US soybean oil use. Biodiesel consumption in 2015 required production use of five billion pounds of soybean oil, or the oil from 441 million soybean bushels. By comparison, fewer than 500 million pounds of soybean oil were needed to meet domestic biodiesel demand in 2005. This shows tremendous growth in market potential over the past decade.[16]

I have been involved in many meetings and trips over the years focused on biodiesel. On one such trip, a group of us from the USSEC went to Indonesia and Malaysia to learn more about palm oil, which is one of the biggest competitors to soybean oil in the world for the vegetable oil market. Indonesia does import a lot of lower-grade soybeans from the United States to make a traditional soy food called tempeh. Soybeans go through a fermentation process that binds them together in a cake form. I tried it, but I did not like it. It was important to stop in Jakarta, Indonesia, and thank the Indonesians for their business and to offer our assistance in future trade relations. Indonesia was looking at biofuel production as a job development and income generator to decrease the poverty among its people.

We next visited with the Palm Oil Producers' Board in Kuala Lumpur, Malaysia. It is interesting that they face many of the same challenges as US soybean farmers. We agreed that there was a growing demand and a good market for both palm and soybean oil.

While in Kuala Lumpur, I received a call from Jeb Bush, whose brother, George W. Bush, had appointed him cochair of an international ethanol commission. President Lula of Brazil had appointed Roberto Rodrigues, Brazil's minister of agriculture, as the other cochair. I knew Minister Rodrigues very well. We had a number of meetings together on the foot and mouth disease eradication effort in South America and also had held a news conference together while I was in Brasilia, the capital of Brazil.

The international ethanol commission was having a meeting in a few days in Miami, Florida, and was inviting agriculture leaders from around the world to visit about biofuels. USB CEO John Becherer and I talked it over with other USB members on the trip and decided I should leave Malaysia the next day and fly to Miami to attend the meeting.

It turned out to be a small group of approximately thirty to thirty-five people at the meeting, mostly ministers of ag and importers of biofuels. I was one of only a few nongovernment officials at the meeting, and the only person to talk on behalf of soy biodiesel. Governor Bush and others asked a lot of questions about biodiesel. The big question, and the reason

I was asked to the meeting, was whether the commission should change and be a biofuels commission, not just an ethanol commission. My answer was, of course, yes. Everyone agreed that biofuels would be a big part of the future of alternative energy around the world.

Picture of news conference in Brasilia. Left to right: *Sebastiao Costa Guedes, director/CEO of the Brazilian National Beef Council and president of GIEFA; Phil, North America private sector representative to GIEFA; Roberto Rodriguez, minister of agriculture of Brazil; Gabriel Alves Maciel, duty minister of agriculture for livestock and food supply in Brazil. (Photo courtesy of Phil Bradshaw.)*

Governor Bush's staff followed up with me a time or two after the meeting, but nothing ever happened. I visited with Minister Rodrigues later, and he said it went "kaput." I know Governor Bush's staff wanted me to support the effort and push it forward, but I just did not have the time to devote to it. I did offer ideas and suggested people that might be able to help, but no progress was made.

I have volunteered many hours to different organizations and checkoff programs. In the end, I hope that my small contribution has helped to benefit not only my fellow farmer, but my fellow consumer in this country and around the world.

The Soybean Soap Opera

I've never been one to watch soap operas (or at least admit that I do!). My life is filled with enough drama. From what little I have seen of them, they tend to focus on money and power and who does and does not have one or the other or both. This causes friction between the characters and leads to interesting storylines. Through my involvement in the soybean organizations, I was caught up in a real-life soap opera, which also revolved around money and power.

A number of the checkoff programs have an option for farmers to request a refund of the checkoff funds collected from the commodity that they sell. These programs are called voluntary checkoff programs and are not as restrictive as those that do not have the right of refund. Those programs that do not have the right to receive a refund are called mandatory checkoff programs. These mandatory checkoff programs cannot do any political or lobbying activities. I have been involved in both types of commodity programs, and there are advantages to both.

A voluntary program has the advantage of using the money raised in almost any manner the governing board chooses to use it, including lobbying and political activities with only limited restrictions. Mandatory national checkoff programs must follow many compliance guidelines and restrictions.

The USDA's Agricultural Marketing Service (AMS) oversees the mandatory national checkoff programs, which are led by boards of small and large producers, importers, and other commodity stakeholders. The secretary of agriculture appoints board members, who were nominated by their peers, to the national checkoff boards. Each commodity group's bylaws handle the selection of the governing board a little differently, but basically all are nominated by producers of the commodity and then appointed by the secretary. The secretary may choose not to appoint the candidate nominated, so in most cases, the producers also nominate an alternate. On a number of occasions, in different commodity groups, the secretary has chosen the alternate instead of the candidate.

The national mandatory checkoff programs are very strict about not doing any political lobbying activities. They are very closely supervised in their activities by AMS, sometimes to the point where it becomes burdensome to the commodity groups. The officers, directors, and staff have to be very careful about what they say and do to make sure it is educational and not political or lobbying.

The commodity groups that were funded by membership dues helped start most, if not all, of the checkoff programs. This would end up creating some problems. The checkoff programs have faced some court battles, some going all the way to the Supreme Court.

The National Pork Producers Council (NPPC) was involved in a court case related to the use of the checkoff dollars collected from the sale of hogs. Secretary of Ag Dan Glickman came to an out of court settlement in March 2001. The settlement agreement, among other things, required a distinct separation between the National Pork Board (NPB), which collected the checkoff funds, and NPPC, the membership organization focused on lobbying. This created the need for complete separation between NPB and NPPC. The National Cattlemen's Beef Association (NCBA) had the same problem and also had lawsuits claiming that it must separate the membership program from the checkoff program.

The out-of-court settlement stated that mandatory checkoff programs had to have a very clear break between the membership side that is supported by dues and does political lobbying, and the checkoff side that is supported by the mandatory checkoff and is not allowed to do any lobbying. Beef, dairy, pork, poultry, and soybeans all had to set up separate organizations to manage the checkoff funds collected. This was not an easy thing for the commodity groups to work through. In the early years,

NPPC, NCBA, and other commodity organizations were the administrators that oversaw all checkoff programs. Now, membership organizations that had worked so hard to establish the national checkoff programs could not use those checkoff funds to support themselves. They not only lost most of their operating funds; it was also difficult to get producers to pay dues to support lobbying and legislation. Farmers did not understand why they paid money to the checkoff and still had to pay membership dues.

The NPPC settlement started one of the biggest battles between the soybean farmer organizations—ASA and the checkoff-funded USB. It almost always causes problems when one group has a lot of money and the other one has very little. When I was on the USB board, this was definitely the case for the USB and ASA. The case brought against NPPC led to changes that required checkoff funds to be administered by a separate board from the membership board. The legislation that initiated the soybean checkoff stated that one-half of the funds collected must remain in the state where they were collected and the other half was sent to USB. USB had the fiduciary responsibility for all funds collected. I think most commodity organizations are operated in a similar fashion.

The membership organizations of pork, beef, soybean, and other commodity groups invested a sizable commitment of time and effort, plus several million dollars, in creating the legislation that established the national commodity checkoff programs. When the checkoff funds had to be administered separately from the membership organization, it was hard for those who had donated many hours of work to establish the checkoff to then be shut out of the administration of those funds. These membership organizations, through their lobbying effort, helped to ensure that close to half of the funds used for the development of international markets were maintained in the USDA budget. This separation was very difficult for all commodity groups, but probably created the most unrest in the soybean industry. Soybeans are the largest percentage and dollar volume of agriculture exports. ASA is one of the strongest and most active lobbying organizations of the commodity groups. It was not easy for the officers, directors, and staff of ASA to accept the fact they were not in charge of the dollars collected by the checkoff that they had worked so hard to establish.

The early leaders of USB saw a benefit to having a very small staff and doing most of their work through contractors. This has proven to be a very successful model but is not followed by all checkoffs. Some checkoff programs have larger staffs and do most of the work on programs and activities in-house. I believe this approach gives the producers much more control of the programs, since they have direct contact with the staff involved in the programs. However, it also has some challenges, as groups can't afford to have experts on staff for every subject.

USB could contract with the experts they needed for a specific project. Which approach is best has been debated by smarter people than me, but I think all the checkoff programs, regardless of how they are operated, have been very beneficial to not only the American farmer but to the American consumer and consumers worldwide.

Early on, USB was contracting with ASA to carry out checkoff programs and activities. ASA was also lobbying the government at both the state and national levels. The simple way to explain what the NPPC lawsuit was all about is that some people thought checkoff funds were making it possible for NPPC to lobby the government, which was not allowed under the law.

As a way to avoid the potential issue, USB decided it should contract with a separate entity that was not involved in lobbying and political activity to conduct the checkoff programs. This created a harsh division in the soybean industry, especially with those who had served on the ASA or USB board of directors. The separation created a have and a have not situation between the two groups, which started to fuel the fire of controversy.

USB continued to fund international programs through ASA. Although this still seemed to create problems, as ASA was still lobbying. The leaderships of ASA and USB began to discuss ways to transfer the international marketing program of ASA to a separate entity. In 2004 USB and ASA worked together to create the USSEC. The USDA was supportive of anything that would further separate the checkoff funds from the membership funds used for lobbying.

When I went on the Illinois Soybean Checkoff Board in 2004, I made a conscious decision to do less lobbying and supporting of political candidates. From 2004 to 2012, I made little to no personal contributions to any candidates, nor did I take any leadership positions in any candidate's campaign as I had in the past. I did, however, still support my local candidates. Because I was serving on the Soybean Checkoff Board, I was careful not to give the impression that I supported any particular candidate or any particular regulation or law being proposed.

During the transition of the move of the international marketing program, ASA and USB both had some good leaders. Unfortunately, many had their own agendas and their own organization's interests at heart. They were very far apart on how to actually make the change.

Neal Bredehoft from Missouri was president of ASA. Neal was a very well-read and stable individual. He was the right man to handle the transition of the international marketing program. He was very firm in his efforts to protect ASA but also knew what was happening with all commodity programs. Greg Anderson from Kansas was chairman of USB and was also well-read and informed on what the courts and USDA were saying about separation of checkoff dollars and lobbying organizations. He also understood the USB board's intentions to transfer the program.

I think both ASA and USB had mixed feeling about how to move forward. Producers on both boards had strong feelings and became entrenched in their positions. For more than fifty years, ASA had been the international marketing arm for soybean farmers. USB had the fiduciary responsibility for the checkoff funds, and it had become clear that farmer checkoff funds could have no connections to lobbying organizations.

Bob Metz from South Dakota was elected president of ASA in December 2005. Bob was a man who wanted to get things done, promote the soybean industry, and help the world. He knew for those things to happen long term there needed to be a strong export market and a strong lobbying organization. Bob and Greg led the two groups in the formation and establishment of the USSEC. The USB board was divided right down the middle over this issue. ASA had been around so long and was so strong in most states that many directors on USB did not see or understand the need for a change in the international marketing program. In a very close vote, the USB board elected Curt Raasch from Iowa as chairman. Curt was elected to bring better relations between ASA and USB and to help ASA keep support from USB and USSEC. This proved that there was still a lot of support for ASA on the USB board. I think Curt's election helped bring support to the agreement for USB to pay ASA for the use of the international logo that ASA had developed. It also brought to USB's attention the need to help resolve ASA's monetary commitment concerning the funding of its pension plan. At some point USB and the state soybean associations agreed to help fund ASA's pension plan.

Eric Niemann from Kansas was the next farmer leader elected chairman of USB, and Richard Ostile from North Dakota was elected president of ASA. I always felt Richard thought there could have been a way to keep ASA running the international marketing program. Dan Duran, who had been hired to be the CEO of USSEC, had become very controversial. At this time, I was serving on the USSEC board representing USB. I felt Dan did some things that people did not support, but overall he had done a good job. He came in with little experience of working with farmers or volunteer boards. Ike Boudreaux from Louisiana was elected chairman of the USB board in December 2007. Ike was a very strong leader but at times was controversial. John Hoffman from Iowa was elected president of ASA. I believed that John thought USB was the worst thing that had ever happened to the soybean industry. Unfortunately, he believed a lot of the rumors and stories going around about USSEC and USB directors. I think John and some directors from ASA and USB thought if USSEC failed, ASA would get the international marketing program back.

USSEC was formed with directors from allied industry—ASA and USB. There was so much mistrust between ASA and USB that the new organization had trouble from day one. Although we were all soybean farmers wanting to help the industry, many individuals had ulterior motives.

I can remember walking down the hall in the Hilton hotel in St. Louis with John Hoffman in December 2008. He said something to the effect that ASA was going to take the gloves off and straighten USB and the whole mess out. My reply was to be careful what you do, because it might do more harm than good. A few hours later, USB was informed that ASA had requested the USDA have the Office of Inspector General (OIG) investigate misuse of checkoff funds. That request went through Senator Charles Grassley from Iowa.

In 2005, shortly after USSEC was formed, ASA had submitted to the OIG a complaint that USB allegedly misused checkoff funds. AMS did a review and did not substantiate the allegations. I knew AMS had done this review and that USB had done a number of reviews and internal audits, so I felt like the OIG would not find any big problems. However, I had heard most of the rumors and seen many of the emails that had been flying around between USB and ASA, so I was not sure what might show up. The OIG officer doing the investigation did not interview me but did ask our attorney if I wanted to make a statement or if I thought I could add anything. I said I had no knowledge other than what I am sure they had heard from other USB directors. I did not send any emails concerning any of the allegations or rumors, nor did I say anything in public.

One of the hardest things for me to deal with was when John Hoffman said in a radio interview that someone with USB had an affair while in Japan. The reporter had me on right after that, and I said USB would immediately address any issues the OIG found. There were some who did not hear the interview clearly and thought I was having an affair with some lady in Japan. Stories got bigger and wilder as emails went around the world.

I thought I understood why most USB chairmen and ASA presidents did and said the things they did. I was always careful to question the action, not the individual. I felt bad because Chuck Myers was chairman of USB in 2009 during the investigation and lost the opportunity to do things that would help the soybean industry. I never felt sorry for Johnny Dobson, president of ASA in 2009, because he helped make the decision to ask for the OIG investigation. John Hoffman, as president of ASA in 2008, could have handled the differences between USB, USSEC, and ASA with a little cooler head.

Rob Joslin from Ohio was elected president of ASA in 2010 at about the same time that I became chairman of USB. Right after I became chairman, Rob drove over and spent the afternoon at my home. Rob was a very concerned and conscientious individual. After our discussion that afternoon, I felt like he was concerned about how the OIG investigation was going to come out. I agreed to sit down with the ASA executive committee and visit with them. It was risky for me, and I knew that, but felt I had to do something to start building more trust between the two organizations. It was a nice discussion. I made no commitments, but I do think it helped to start the healing process between the two groups. Some directors of USB felt ASA should just go away, but most knew it would not. Even though I took a real good chewing from my USB executive committee for sitting down with ASA, I felt it was a good move to start building trust between the two organizations.

On July 23, 2010, after spending eighteen months reviewing thousands of documents and interviewing numbers of individuals, OIG released its report to Senator Charles Grassley. The report stated, "We found insufficient evidence to support ASA's allegations, but we do recommend closer oversight by USB of USSEC in the future."[17]

The day the report was released; a number of USB officers and staff were on the way to Mexico. We knew that the press would want to do interviews and that we wanted to get the results out to the public as soon as we could. USB staff set up a news conference at the Dallas airport, where we could give statements and answer questions. I made a general statement as chairman of USB saying we were pleased with the findings, and we had felt confident all along. I was very careful not to say anything negative about ASA, even though some USB directors thought I should tell how much it had cost the soybean farmers and how much stress it had caused directors, officials, and staff of USB, USSEC, and USDA.

A number of individuals felt like they had been hurt by comments and emails. I had made up my mind long before the report came out that there was nothing to be gained by speaking ill of ASA, its directors, or staff. No one knew what the report was going to say, so we had discussions with attorneys and others on what action the board might take under different scenarios. I felt like we knew what our public statement was going to be under different scenarios. I wanted to say that I had warned John Hoffman back in St. Louis in 2008 to be careful what he did, but I stuck with my core belief of nothing to be gained by criticizing anyone or any organization. My mother always told me, "It is always too early to criticize and never too late to say thank you."

I would like to think that during this time of turmoil, my contribution was to begin the healing process by agreeing to meet with the ASA president and the executive committee and to only respond in a positive manner to the results of the investigation. There will always be disagreements between organizations, but a little trust and cooperation goes a long way. Now, several years later, relations have improved between ASA and USB, and they are working closely together. In the end this soybean soap opera had a happy ending!

Trips to Russia and China

A Chinese proverb says, "May you live in interesting times." While this may sound like a blessing, it is actually a curse that means may you experience much disorder and trouble in your life. There have been many times throughout history when we could say we were living in interesting times. The 1970s were an interesting time for me, as well as the country and world, as I had the opportunity to travel to two communist countries and be involved in trips that would lay the groundwork for future trade relations.

In 1971 the Soviet Union purchased three million tons of feed grains from the United States; part of the sale was 440 million bushels of wheat. This purchase amounted to approximately 30 percent of our country's total wheat production. This purchase sent grain prices skyrocketing and fueled expansion in the agriculture sector. The large grain sale to America's number one nemesis of the Cold War was unsettling to many people. It was referred to by many as the "Great Grain Robbery." At that time there was a subsidy on commodities sold to foreign customers in order to encourage exports of US grain and to reduce the large supplies of domestic corn, soybeans, and wheat. The grain companies making the sale to the Soviet Union had received large subsidies from the US government. This caused many politicians to question this trade policy. Secretary of State Henry Kissinger called his counterpart, Agriculture Secretary Earl Butz, and snapped at Butz, "We have not gotten out of this grain situation what we should have."[18]

Earl Butz was the secretary of agriculture under President Richard

Nixon. Secretary Butz visited with Congressman Paul Findley, and they decided the United States should have a trade delegation team go to the Soviet Union to review the large grain sale and determine how to better handle sales in the future. They began making plans for pulling together a team of individuals to visit the communist country.

At the time I was president of the Illinois Pork Producers Association (IPPA) and a leader of the Farmers for Findley for Congress. Paul asked me to go on the trip with him to the Soviet Union.

The IPPA agreed to pay part of my expenses, and I agreed to pay the rest. I was very excited to go. It was a very unique experience to visit the Soviet Union in the midst of the Cold War.

Fifteen people, mostly from Illinois, were part of the trade delegation team that went to Russia in September 1972.

Members of the 1972 trade delegation to Russia. Phil is pictured on the stairs, third from left. *(Photo courtesy of Phil Bradshaw.)*

Members of the group included Gordon Ropp, Illinois director of agriculture; Harold Steele, president of the Illinois Farm Bureau; Congressman Paul Findley; James F. Seeley, Governor Oglivie's assistant—Washington, DC, office; Robert Gilmore, director of the National Livestock Feeders Association; Harold Kuehn, president of the American Soybean Association; George Bicknell, executive vice president of Farmers Export Co.; Dwight Davis, director of foreign trade—Illinois Farm Bureau; John P. Doherty, vice president of operations—Illinois Grain Corporation; Richard Feltner, University of Illinois—head of the Department of Agricultural Economics; Ken Hartweg, Funks Seeds International Inc.; Jim Stewart, De Kalb Ag Research, Inc.—Poultry Division; Robert Osborn, export officer—Brussels, Belgium—Illinois Trade Office; and James Tippett, Illinois Farm Bureau News Service director. I was definitely the lowest-ranking member of the delegation.

When we arrived at the Moscow airport, we were greeted by representatives from the US embassy. As we drove from the airport to our hotel, we stopped where the Russians had fought to the death and blocked the German army from advancing into Moscow during World War II. It was hard to believe the bloodshed that had occurred on the very spot that we were standing.

We stayed at the Rasscia hotel, which was located near Red Square. After a brief meeting with the group and eating supper, I went to my room to get some sleep after the long trip. I remember giving the gentleman who took my bags to my room a ballpoint pen that IPPA gave me to hand out to people on my trip. The pen had a little red pig on top of it.

Shortly after lying down in my bed there was a knock on my door. I assumed it was one of the members of the delegation team. I got up and went to the door, but no one responded when I asked who it was. I decided someone must have knocked on the wrong door and went back to bed. It was not very long until I heard a knock again. I got up and asked who was there, but no one answered. We had been told to expect our rooms to be bugged, so the Soviets could hear everything we said. By this time my mind was dreaming up all kinds of possibilities of what might be happening. Was the KGB out to get this farmer from Pike County? I wedged a chair in front of the door for added security and to help wake me if someone tried to bust into my room.

I went back to bed for the third time, and again came the knock on my door. Now this time I was upset and in a very loud voice I said, "Who is it?" From the other side of the door came a sweet little voice in Russian. This didn't sound like a member of the KGB, so I opened the door. It was the lady who was in charge of the floor at the hotel. She had seen me give the ballpoint pen to the man, and she motioned like writing. I decided she wanted a pen. When I got a pen out and handed it to her, she had a big smile, and I know she said thanks in Russian many times. It was a good move on my part because from then on she was my friend and always gave me a big smile and an extra bath towel.

We had many interesting meetings with Russian officials. One night the delegation was split up and went to different dinner functions. Seven of us went south of Moscow to a feed mill and eight of us went north of Moscow to a livestock research farm. The interesting thing was both groups had the exact same dinner with almost the same toasts and remarks made by the Russians, even though we were almost two hundred miles apart. This was the night they tried to get us all drunk on vodka.

Congressman Findley kept toasting with water. Paul never drank alcohol. I only took a small sip of vodka each time, but soon both Americans and Russians started teasing me about not drinking enough. So, to avoid a big international crisis, I drank an entire water glass full of vodka.

I had consumed very little alcohol in my life, but that night I succumbed to the peer pressure. When we got back to the hotel, I took a cold shower and then went out with some of the guys to look around Moscow. I did not feel well the next day.

Being the lowest ranking member of the fifteen-person team, I did not attend some of the high-level meetings. One day while the rest of the group was in a meeting, I went with the lady who was our translator to do some sightseeing. We went on a tour of the Moscow exhibit of economic achievement. An older lady showed us the Russians' first Sputnik satellite that went into space ahead of the US space exploration. She told the two of us, "Never let your country be weak and have to defend itself with so little, as we had to do when we stopped the German army." She said that every member of her family was killed as they defended Moscow with everything that they had, including clubs, knives, and pitchforks.

Before I left for Moscow, the Central Intelligence Agency (CIA) contacted me and gave me a small 110 camera. They asked me to take a lot of pictures as we traveled around in the Soviet Union. This was as close to being a spy as I ever was. I took that little camera everywhere I went and took a lot of pictures whenever I had the opportunity. Before I left the Soviet Union, I went to a debriefing room in the US embassy and went through the pictures with those at the embassy. I don't think that I caught anything too secret on the film, but they seemed pleased with what I had done.

Overall the trip was a success. The delegation made some of the same recommendations an earlier group had made to President Kennedy. Our main recommendation was that when dealing with central governments, such as the Soviet Union, one US company should do all the negotiating and then all the companies share in the sale.

As if going to one major communist country wasn't enough, I had an opportunity to travel to another communist world power. While the United States was dealing with the Soviet Union and the Cold War, the Nixon administration was working on normalization of relationships with China. In the early 1970s, private discussions began between the United States and China. Then on April 10, 1971, a team of US Ping-Pong players visited China to play against the Chinese Ping-Pong team. Ping-Pong diplomacy was under way. This trip set the stage for President Nixon to become the first president to ever visit China.

President Nixon and Henry Kissinger, who was the special assistant to the president at the time, signed the Shanghai communiqué on February 28, 1972, Nixon's last day of his historic trip to China. In my opinion the communiqué between the United States and the People's Republic of China that pledged it was in the best interest of both countries to work toward normal relationships greatly benefitted US agriculture because it opened up the world's largest group of consumers to our products. It took seven years to fully implement the agreement.

Mao Zedong was the chairman of the Communist Party of China. Mao proclaimed the start of the People's Republic of China in 1949 and led the country through many reforms and disastrous policies. Chairman Mao initiated the Cultural Revolution in 1966 to rid the country of impure elements and reestablish his authority. The Gang of Four was in control of the Communist Party of China during that time. The Gang of Four consisted of Chairman Mao's wife, plus three other high-ranking Chinese officials. The Cultural Revolution ended when Chairman Mao died in 1976, and Deng Xiaoping took over as ruler of the Communist Party in China. The United States and China started working again toward normalization. Even though the Shanghai Communiqué was signed in February 1972, and the two countries had exchanged liaison officers and opened offices—the United States in Beijing and China in Washington, DC—little else happened until the end of the Cultural Revolution.

My friend Congressman Findley had always been a very open-minded individual and thought the United States should visit and have relationships with many other countries. The first time I heard Paul Findley say we should develop relations with the People's Republic of China was in 1966. At that time a fourth of all the people on the planet lived in China. He thought, and I agreed, that you cannot ignore that many people without it causing you big problems.

Paul served in Congress in the early 1970s with George H. Bush. I had an opportunity to meet Mr. Bush on one of my trips to DC. Mr. Bush was appointed the first liaison officer to China. One of the articles in the communiqué called for expanded people-to-people contact between the two countries.

The new Communist Party chairman, Deng Xiaoping, wanted to improve the living standards for his people. China did not have enough food to feed its one billion people. The first thing Chairman Deng Xiaoping wanted from the United States was agriculture technology and advice. As a result, George H. Bush, as the liaison officer to China, contacted Congressman Findley about his desire to have US agriculture leaders travel to China. Bush wanted a group to see China's agriculture and discuss how the two countries could work together to increase food production and trade. The Chinese liaison officer and government were receptive to the idea.

Since Congressman Findley was a ranking Republican on the House Foreign Affairs Committee and represented an agricultural district, it made him a logical choice to put together a trip of farm leaders to China. I wasn't on a state ag board at the time, but I had helped Paul organize this trip, so he asked me to go along. I was honored to be asked to go on the first major agricultural trip to China since World War II. I was very willing to pay my own way.

Members of the 1978 trade mission trip to China. Phil is pictured in the front row, fourth from right. *(Photo courtesy of Phil Bradshaw.)*

Eighteen people were selected to go on the trip. They were all farm leaders of organizations and companies located in Illinois. Those who went on the trip were: Congressman Paul Findley; Congressman Edward Madigan; John Block, Illinois director of agriculture; Harold Steele, president of Illinois Farm Bureau; Harold Dodd, president of Illinois Farmers Union; Dr. Orville Bentley, dean, College of Agriculture University of Illinois; Allen Aves, vice president of the American Soybean Association; Hans Becherer, vice president of Deere and Company; Carrol Bolen, president of Illinois and Wisconsin Division of Pioneer Hi-Bred; James Lilly, editor, *Prairie Farmer* magazine; John R. Nelsen, vice president of Animal Sciences, DeKalb Ag Research; Orion Samuelson, farm news editor, WGN-TV and radio; Donald Duster, director of the Department of Business and Economic Development for Illinois; Harold Champeau, Foreign Agriculture Affairs officer, USDA; Craig Findley, editor and photographer, *Gazette Times*; William W. Allen, executive director of information, Illinois Farm Bureau; Robert Wichser, administrative assistant to Congressman Findley; and myself, Philip E. Bradshaw, past president of the Illinois Pork Producers Association.

The Chinese liaison officer in Washington, DC, and George H. Bush invited the whole team to DC to the Chinese liaison complex, now the Chinese embassy, for a visit and a briefing in January before we went to China. Health officials required us to take a number of shots before we could travel to China.

In March 1978 the group met in a VIP room at O'Hare Airport in Chicago before boarding the plane to Japan. Upon arriving in Chicago, officials checked to make sure that we had our necessary paperwork and required shot records. Congressman Ed Madigan from Illinois was the minority leader of the House Ag Committee and was joining the group to China. Congressman Madigan did not get his shots before he showed up at O'Hare. He told the nurse that he did not need the shots, but the nurse told him that if he did not get the shots he would be quarantined when he returned from China. I had to laugh to myself, because Madigan was a large man, and this nurse was probably not more than five feet tall. In my opinion Ed Madigan liked to use the fact that he was a congressman to impress people and get his way, but that young nurse was not going to back down or give in.

Congressman Madigan ended up getting several shots that morning before we left on our nonstop flight to Tokyo. When we arrived in Japan, I think Congressman Madigan was feeling pretty bad. He went to the embassy infirmary and back to the hotel, and as I remember, he missed most all of the activities with Japan's ambassador and the agricultural leaders from Japan.

US airlines were not allowed to land in or fly over China at that time, so we took Japan Air Lines from Tokyo to Shanghai. Once in China all our flights were on Chinese airlines.

We flew from Shanghai to Beijing, where we stayed at one of the nicest hotels in Beijing. We traveled extensively throughout eastern China. We went as far north as Changchum in the Jilin Province and as far south as Guangzhuo and out of China into Hong Kong. In 1978 Hong Kong was still part of the British Empire.

Most of our time was spent talking about agriculture and trade. We visited with a number of very high-level governmental and agricultural officials plus toured a number of farms throughout China. I liked the food and the people. A few things I noticed right away were that there were no birds and there was no trash. Also, there were bicycles everywhere, as most people used bicycles as their main mode of transportation.

I had heard people claim that many of the Chinese people looked alike. I found that to be true. Everyone in China in 1978 wore what I called the Mao blue uniform. Every man that I saw had his hair cut above their ears, and every woman had her hair cut just below her ears. It was odd to see millions of people all dressed in what looked like coveralls with similar haircuts.

We stayed in nice hotels and had cars with drivers to drive us wherever we needed to go. We made quite a scene as we drove around in our cars with American flags on the front. On some days, when people knew we were coming to their town, thousands would be standing along the streets, just to get a glimpse of an American. Most Chinese people had not seen an American before. They did not want to see me as much as Orion Samuelson or Allen Aves, who were both over six feet tall.

We saw the Great Wall, Ming tombs, and the Forbidden City. We also saw the remains of Chairman Mao entombed in a glass vault at Tiananmen Square. I have seen three communist rulers entombed in glass—Vladimir Lenin in Moscow, Ho Chi Minh Ha Noi in Vietnam, and Mao.

The group wanted to present an agriculture-related gift to the Chinese. Since pork production was an important part of the Chinese culture, I helped line up one of the best boars in the United States to be shipped to China. I found out later that the boar got a disease and died a few months later. Despite this, the Chinese were very appreciative of our gift.

After spending three weeks in China, we met in Hong Kong with US and other world leaders plus the press to give a report on our trip. I can remember Paul Findley saying in that press conference: "China will purchase over $1 billion of US products in the future." Today they purchase approximately 25 percent of all the soybeans produced in the United States, which amounts to more than $8 billion annually from just one commodity.

I was not a leader or a spokesman for the group, as I was more like an assistant to Congressman Findley. I was not asked to speak at the news conference or meetings. Congressman Findley, Congressman

Madigan, and Illinois Director of Agriculture John Block were the primary spokespersons.

China is a
top 3 export market for
U.S. and Illinois agriculture

China has nearly **1.4 billion consumers**
while the U.S. has only **325 million consumers**

1.38 billion

325 million

In 2017, U.S. farmers exported
$22.5 billion
in ag products to China

China is Illinois' largest export partner accounting for **25%** of all Illinois agriculture exports

The U.S-China trade relationship supports **2.6 million jobs** in the United States

Illinois farmers export to China:

$1.75 billion soybeans	more than **$500 million** corn*	**$100 million** sorghum	**$50 million** pork	**$300,000** beef

*incudes corn, ethanol, and DDGS

Infographic on China and Illinois agriculture courtesy of Illinois Farm Bureau® copyright 2018.

One thing about John Block that I found interesting was that he jogged every morning while we were on the trip. To my knowledge he was the only member of the group to have acupuncture while we were in China. He also recorded many of the meetings, while most of us tried to keep notes with pen and paper. John Block, a West Point graduate, is one of the most capable men I think I have ever met. He always knew what to say, when to say it, and where to be.

The trips to Russia and China were widely publicized and were watched closely by the ag community across the United States. As president of IPPA at the time of the Russian trip, I was known to many in the pork industry. I was invited to speak all over the Midwest about the trips. I was not paid for giving most of the speeches, but I did enjoy the opportunity to share my experiences. I received many requests from different groups, such as Rotary Clubs, Lions Clubs, Chambers of Commerce, and Farm Bureau groups, to speak about my trips. One of my neighbors, Greg Carnes, had a Mooney Executive airplane that he didn't get to fly that often. I would give him money for fuel and the expense of the plane, and he would fly me all over the Midwest to give speeches about my trips to Russia and China, as well as other activities that I was involved in at the time.

The Mooney was a small single-engine four-passenger plane. It would fly 175 to 200 miles per hour. One time I can remember stopping the corn planter at 5:00 p.m. and being at a dinner meeting to speak in northern Illinois by 7:15 p.m. We had a lot of interesting times in that little plane. When Greg first started flying me, we would land at a small, private, oil and chip runway near Pittsfield with one light at each end. If someone forgot to turn on the lights, it made for a difficult landing. I can remember a number of times late at night looking for landmarks, such as the Shell gas station and the roller rink lights to help guide us home. Fortunately, Pittsfield later built a nice airport.

One time I was asked to speak at an all-day and night event in southern Illinois. I was on the program in the morning and again that evening, so they offered to get me a room for the night. The group wanted to know if it would be okay with me to share a room. I said it was okay as long as there were two beds. I had to be home early the next morning to take care of the pigs, so I went to bed early. About 1:00 a.m. my roommate came into the room and got in bed with me. Now I am not a large man, but you can still see if I am in the bed. I decided to leave right away and was home by 4:00 a.m. I have never shared a room since!

The trips to Russia and China were a highlight for me personally, but they were also a highlight for agriculture. They allowed a closer look behind the Communist curtain and an opportunity to meet people in these countries. Looking back, these definitely were interesting times for me and for our country.

Working to Save the Local Bank

Over the years I have realized that getting through the tough times only makes you stronger. There were no tougher times in my farming career than the farm crisis of the 1980s. During that time US farmers were faced with an economic crisis more severe than any since the Great Depression. More farmers lost their farms in that decade than almost all the other years put together. It was heartbreaking to see so many farmers go broke and be forced to sell what they had worked so hard to achieve.

There were many causes of the economic crisis, and it was many years in the making. After World War II, farmers saw great advances in technology on the farm with improved machinery, seeds, pesticides, and fertilizers, which all led to greater productivity. In the 1950s and '60s, the American farmers' biggest concern was how to get rid of their large surplus of grain. Then along came the 1970s, which resulted in a huge increase in the demand for grains and greatly reduced the large surpluses. This resulted in skyrocketing prices for commodities, and farmers responded by taking on debt to expand their farms and increase production.

In 1979 the Federal Reserve tightened its monetary policy in an attempt to reduce inflation. As a result, interest rates rose to levels not seen since the Civil War. The prime lending rate soared from an average of 6.75 percent in 1976 to where some banks had an all-time high of 21.5 percent in 1980.[19] The impact of the Federal Reserve's decision was felt throughout the US economy, but its effect on farm families and rural banks was especially severe.

Then the straw that broke the camel's back was when President Jimmy Carter halted grain shipments to the Soviet Union in 1980 in response to Russia's invasion of Afghanistan. Commodity prices collapsed, and farmers who had high debt loads were among the first to go out of business.

I started building a new hog confinement building in the fall of 1979. I went to the local bank and told them that I was going to need $100,000. They told me to come in and borrow what I needed as I needed it. At that time interest rates had gone up a little and were around 8 percent. This was not good, but I could still make it work. When I borrowed the last of the money for the building, the interest rate had jumped to more than 15 percent. The highest rate I ever paid was 18 percent, but some farmers paid as high as 21 percent interest.

During this time of extremely high interest rates, it made little difference how good a farmer you were, if you did not have your interest rate locked in. You could have the highest yields in the county, but because of the high interest rates, not be able to pay the bills. Very few people had a rate locked in because the government had kept rates around 6 percent for decades. The rocketing interest rates caught many people off guard. Most farmers who made it through the 1980s did so because they or their family had a high percent of equity and likely had the farm paid off.

The farm crisis soon became the rural crisis as the effect trickled down through the rural economy. When farmers could not pay their bills, many ag businesses also went broke. This led to many people losing their jobs and not being able to pay for their homes, cars, and other necessities.

Land values dropped by half. Land that had been selling for $1,500 an acre was selling for $600 to $700 per acre. The Federal Land Bank had numerous farms for sale. Banks had to start calling loans, which put more land on the market and forcing prices of land down even further. People who had money to invest could get between 15 and 16 percent on a certificate of deposit at the bank, so they were not interested in buying land. Many banks were forced to sell out as they lost their assets, deposits, and loans.

The only reason our farm made it through the 1980s was because we had the interest rate set at 6 percent on the contract for deed from Uncle Clyde and Aunt Dorothy. We had also been very careful not to overspend and were frugal with our money. Linda and I always drove nice cars, but most of the seven cars we have owned each lasted us ten years and had more than two hundred thousand miles. We also didn't have to own the most expensive car on the lot. The same was true for the machinery and equipment that we purchased. We also saved money by building all of our hog buildings ourselves until the hog building that we built in 2003.

The local bank got caught up in the rural depression and had repossessed the local cooperative slaughter and locker plant. Dr. Richard Hull, DVM, and I purchased the old building and equipment from the bank. We employed John Dipple, who had a master's degree in meat science from Purdue. We owned it for twenty years but never made money on our investment. However, we were able to provide a needed service to the community and employed five to eight people through the years. I wish that we would not have sold it because the man who purchased the facility took the equipment and abandoned the old building. It is a service that is needed today in this area.

The rural depression of the 1980s put a number of banks in rural America in a poor capital position. There were more than sixteen hundred bank failures between 1980 and 1994, which was more than at any other time since the event of the Federal Deposit Insurance Corporation in the 1930s.[20]

I'm proud to say that the Farmer National Bank, with total assets of only $12 million, in my hometown of Griggsville, Illinois, was not one of those sixteen hundred banks to close. Dr. Richard Hull was president of the board and was not going to let that happen. Doc Hull and I had already purchased the old locker plant for more than anyone else would give, which, since he was the president of the board, had to be approved by the Office of Controller of Currency (OCC).

Doc Hull spoke to me about becoming involved in the bank but could not say too much because I was not a director or even a stockholder at the time. He did say the bank was kind of a mess, which I already had an idea that it was having a hard time. Two of the bank board members were original board members from when the bank started in 1943. One of the other board members, Mr. Dick Myers, also asked me if I could help keep the bank from being forced to sell. I said I would do what I could, but since I owned no stock in the bank, I could not be a director.

My father, Tom, had five shares and said he would sell them to me because he needed the money. Uncle Clyde also had five shares, but he had already done so much for me that I hated to ask him to sell. Mr. Myers and Doc Hull both said something to Clyde, and he was very willing to sell his stock for a decent price. I had the limit borrowed from the bank, so I had to get money from a neighboring bank to purchase the stock. I found out later that I paid about 10 to 20 percent more for the stock than others had paid about the same time. Even though I paid more for my stock in the bank, over the years it has been a worthy investment as the stock greatly increased in value.

The bank board of directors officially seated me on the board on the first Wednesday of February 1982 at 11:00 a.m. The OCC examiners came to the bank at 1:00 p.m. with a list of possible buyers. Doc Hull and I asked them to give us thirty days to see what we could do to improve the bank's financial situation. I remember very clearly the examiners asking the board if they were going to put in more capital, and no one said yes.

Boatman's Bank in St. Louis was our bank's clearing bank. That seemed like a logical place to start in order to learn what we needed to do to keep our bank locally owned. It just so happened that William Trotter (Bucky) Bush was the president and CEO of Boatman's Bank. I had met his brother, George H. Bush, on a few occasions over the years, while he was in Congress and while he was in the liaison office to China and director of the CIA. The next day I called Mr. Bucky Bush and told him about the bank and my going on the board. I was very pleased with his friendliness and helpfulness. I remember telling him that I knew his brother George, and he said, "A lot of people know my brother." George Bush was the vice president of the United States at the time.

Bucky referred me to his vice president for branch banks and said he knew about our little town and had been to Griggsville and remembered seeing all of the purple martin birdhouses. Griggsville claims to be the "Purple Martin Capital of the Nation" with numerous birdhouses lining the streets of the town, including a 562-apartment bird high-rise that reaches a height of seventy feet. The last thing he said was if we had any problems to call him back. He assured me that we would not have to close or sell our bank.

Doc Hull and I set up a time to meet with the bank vice president, and we went down to St. Louis and met him. He had already done his homework and had a plan. The plan was simple. If we did not have or want to add capital, then we'd have to shrink the bank's total assets. We could not do a lot of downsizing, since there was only $12 million of assets to start with. He had three suggestions: get a big accounting firm to come in and go through the bank's books and records and set up a good accounting system for the bank, do a 100 percent verification of all customers of the bank, and hire a consulting firm to come in and help get the bank back on track.

Some of the directors and employees thought we were out of our minds when we hired Arthur Anderson, one of the largest accounting firms in the country, to come and work with our little bank. We knew we had to improve our bank's records and bookkeeping. A local firm could have done that, but examiners would not have known if they were a good accounting firm, just cheap, or maybe a buddy to someone associated with the bank.

Boatman's sent three of its field staff to the bank to help review accounts. After going through nearly two thousand accounts, not one had a serious problem. I was asked to rent a post office box so anyone who did not agree with the bank's records could reply to that box. There were a few people who replied and came into the bank with differences, but the differences concerned dates, not money. It was a big relief to know the bank was well managed and there were no signs of fraud. The record keeping was not a modern system, but it was correct.

As the audit was conducted, it was determined that most of the bank's loans were just signed notes with little or no documentation. The field staff asked us what we could tell them about each loan. We basically classified loans as red, yellow, and green. If red, we would ask the borrower to come into the bank and give us more information. If they did not have any property to guarantee the loan, we told them to find another lender or pay off the loan. If yellow, we would ask them to stop by the bank to talk with us and ask for more collateral before they borrowed any more money from the bank. Then if green, you heard nothing from us until the borrower came in, and then we talked about getting up-to-date financial information.

A number of the bank's borrowers moved their loans and deposits to other banks, which lowered the bank's total assets to approximately $10 million. This in turn raised the bank's capital to asset percentage and also decreased the bank's potential for loan losses. This was enough to satisfy the OCC and help get the bank headed in the right direction.

For those of you who are used to dealing with large banks, remember we are talking about a $12 million bank in a town of twelve hundred people. Every depositor or borrower doing business with the Farmers National Bank of Griggsville was well-known by most directors and employees. Directors and employees knew where the borrower or depositor worked, lived, who he or she was related to, and what the person did in his or her spare time. They knew where the farm was, how many acres of crops were planted, where the farmer purchased his supplies, and where he sold his grain and livestock. All of the records and information were not needed until the financial world changed, and interest rates went through the roof.

Farmers and general borrowers could not make payments if they did not have a high equity position. In the 1980s a farmer could be the best farmer ever, but if he did not have at least 50 percent equity or have his interest rate locked in, he could not meet his obligations. Nor could the average worker make his or her payments on the same income as when the rates were 6 percent.

It took a lot of work and support from many people over almost a decade, but Farmers National Bank came out of its weak position and now has three locations with $84 million in assets and twenty-two employees and has a very strong capital base with good earnings.

I served on the bank board from 1981 to 2008 and was chairman part of that time. One of my proudest accomplishments in my career is helping to keep our local bank from closing or being forced to sell and helping it grow to what it is today.

18

Interstate Highway and New Philadelphia

Americans have always had a fascination with the open road. The wind in your hair, or in my case the wind on my bare head, driving across the country to see America. As nostalgic as Route 66 is and makes for good memories, our country would not be the superpower that we are without the interstate highway system. The development of interstate highways connected our country from coast to coast and border to border. This improved our national defense by being able to transport troops and equipment, while providing drivers with safer and quicker routes to travel and improved commerce.

The interstate system was one of the greatest public works projects ever attempted. While it has benefited the public as a whole, it came at a cost to many private landowners. As you're driving down the interstate, you probably don't think that someone else used to own the land that the road is on now. The interstate impacted rural America in many ways. One of the main ways was changing the landscape by cutting farm fields into smaller fields, demolishing homes and businesses, and going around towns. Deciding where all the actual roads would go would lead to many heated debates and confrontations. I experienced this firsthand, but as with many of life's journeys, you never know where a road might lead you.

One day at lunch in 1981, my old buddy Carl Krusa from Scott County on the east side of the Illinois River called me and said, "What are you going to do about this interstate highway? You know all those politicians." Carl reminded me that I owed him one after his request for help about the pseudorabies disease. He mentioned that a recent lawsuit would require the Illinois Department of Transportation (IDOT) to move the proposed route of the interstate highway and bridge right next to his new house, which he had built to get away from the original proposed route. He said that the new proposed route would angle across the river bottom making three corner fields on both sides of the river. I told him that I would look into it and see what I could do. That was the beginning of my involvement in an eleven-year struggle on an interstate highway being built in the middle of West Central Illinois, also known as "FORGOTONIA."

IDOT had built I-72, known as the Central Illinois Expressway, from Champaign, Illinois, to just north of Winchester, Illinois, using mostly federal dollars. At the time the interstate ended on the east side of the Illinois River. The Illinois Farm Bureau supported West Central Illinois needing a four-lane highway and new bridge over the Illinois River and talked with other civic leaders about the need for it. This was one of the last interstate highways proposed to be built under President Eisenhower's plan.

President Eisenhower was a strong proponent of improving the nation's roadways by developing an interstate system of highways that would improve traffic safety, increase commerce, and provide for the movement of military troops and supplies in the event of a catastrophe or during a time of war. Congress passed the Federal Aid Highway Act of 1954, which authorized $175 million for an interstate system. Eisenhower kept pushing for a more comprehensive interstate network of highways, which became a reality when he signed the Federal-Aid Highway Act of 1956.

Sam and Juliet Wade, a brother and sister, owned a small farm on the west side of the Illinois River, where the proposed highway was going to be built. They had filed a lawsuit to stop the building of the highway and the two bridges, one for the westbound traffic and one for the eastbound traffic. Mr. David Ader, a Chicago attorney, was hired by the Wades for a small retainer fee. He filed an eight-count lawsuit in US District Court in Chicago against both the US and Illinois Departments of Transportation. The case was assigned to Judge Herbert Will, and he issued a hold on all construction of the highway and work on the bridges. Mr. Ader presented an alternative route for the highway through the little town of Valley City, Illinois, and right past Carl and Janet Krusa's house.

The alternate route was displayed in the local papers, and it immediately became an agricultural issue. Farmers had worked with IDOT to route the highway in a way to minimize the impact to their land. Now the proposed alternate route had thrown all that work and planning out the window. Farmers, like the Krusa family, had built buildings and changed fields and fences in preparation of the highway going on the agreed route. The Pike County Farm Bureau called a meeting asking civic, political, farm, and business leaders, and interested individuals from all over West Central Illinois and Northeast Missouri to attend. There was standing room only in the Pike County Farm Bureau hall. I was elected to chair the meeting.

Those in attendance made important decisions and recommended the next steps in the process. One of the main suggestions was for residents from Adams, Pike, Scott, and Morgan Counties in Illinois to form a group to work to get the highway back on the original route and back on the proposed timeline. It was recommended for the group to be made up of people from all four counties and raise money to hire a law firm to represent the community's interest. I was asked to organize the group, and each county was asked to suggest names of people from their county to serve. David Nuessen, the mayor of Quincy, recommended names from Adams County. Jacksonville Mayor Milt Hocking suggested names from Morgan County. Gary Ralston, vice president of Consolidated Grain and Barge (CGB), recommended names from Scott County. Those of us from Pike County collectively agreed on five individuals, which gave us more representation than the other counties. This was all right with everyone because more people from Pike County were going to be affected by changing the route than the other counties.

An Illinois not for profit corporation was formed and used the name AMPS, which stood for Adams, Morgan, Pike, and Scott counties. There were many ideas on how to move forward, but the one thing we all agreed on was to get Judge Will to lift the injunction and let the bridges be built over the Illinois River. This meant we had to have a good legal team.

Gary Ralston and his boss, Bob Frane, president and CEO of CGB, provided AMPS with their in-house attorney, Stuart Zimbalist. Several of AMPS's first meetings were held in the CGB office in Naples, Illinois. In addition to the AMPS board, other political and transportation officials attended the meetings, including Illinois Secretary of Transportation John Kramer, Illinois Chief Highway Engineer Harold Monroney, Quincy Highway Committee Chairman Tom Oakley, and Missouri Highway Transportation Commissioner Tom Boland.

Stuart was an energetic individual and very dedicated to Bob and the CGB team. He immediately started looking for a law firm to represent AMPS and the citizens of West Central Illinois and Northeast Missouri in the lawsuit. We agreed to hire the law firm of Mayor, Brown, and Plate in Chicago. They assigned Wayne Waylan and Percy Angelo as the lead attorneys on the case. They reviewed all of the court hearings, attorney's briefs, and court actions. Ty Fahner, the Illinois Attorney General, had assigned some good but inexperienced young attorneys to defend the state and federal transportation departments.

A week or two after Mayor, Brown, and Plate had taken on the case, Wayne came to visit the site and to see where the highway and bridges were to be built. We had a meeting that day at my home to discuss possible steps to move the case forward. One suggested legal action was for AMPS to intervene and become part of the lawsuit to help defend the Departments of Transportation's position. We filed a motion to intervene, but Judge Will denied it. He said the case had been going on too long to let our group intervene. Wayne had said that might be the ruling, so we filed a friend of the court brief that explained why all eight counts were not valid reasons to stop the construction of the bridges. Judge Will did dismiss six of the eight counts.

One of the two counts Judge Will did not dismiss pertained to the funding of the new bridges. The funding for the new bridges was coming from federal bridge replacement funds. The state of Illinois was spending several million dollars to repair the old bridge for US Route 36, located three miles from the proposed new bridges. It was very clear to all of us that you could not say the new Central Illinois Expressway bridges were going to replace the old bridge when the state was rebuilding the old bridge and had no plans to take it down.

Wayne also said the Federal Department of Transportation had not done a 4(f) study, which is a federal requirement to prove that there were no other prudent or feasible places to build the highway without going through public land. The highway was going through the Pike County conservation area owned by the state. Mayor, Brown, and Plate advised our group to ask the Department of Transportation to do the 4(f) study showing why the only prudent and feasible location was the original route they had planned to build the bridges and highway. They also advised us to look for other financial sources to fund the new bridges.

We visited with Illinois Governor Jim Thompson, Tom Oakley, and Tom Boland to get their ideas on how to move forward. The AMPS board decided to move forward on all fronts. We filed a friend of the court brief, provided legal advice, and helped the Illinois attorney general legal team by providing legal counsel to defend the state and federal departments of transportation. We also asked Congressman Findley and Congressman Bob Michel and Senators Percy and Dixon to introduce legislation to authorize the use of bridge replacement funds to build the bridges. Richard Durbin was elected to Congress in 1982 and was also very supportive of the legislation and the overall effort.

After five years of mediation and studies, the 4(f) document was signed off on by both federal and state authorities. Several agencies had to sign off on the study, including the Department of Interior, EPA, and Department of Transportation. Judge Will lifted the injunction after the state and federal governments agreed to the 4(f) study and the mediation. The out-of-court settlement agreement included several compromises, including using colored concrete for the retaining wall along the highway, so it would look more natural, the narrowing of the highway with no center median across the Wade farm, and a scenic easement along the west riverbank next to the conservation area. The funding for the bridges was approved by the US House and Senate, and President Reagan signed the bill authorizing the funding. The highway was built as originally planned with minimal damage to the surrounding farms.

A few continued to oppose the highway and bridges by claiming damage to bald eagle, Indiana bat, and migratory bird habitats. However, studies showed that the new highway route posed no danger to bald eagles or

Indiana bats and that the route would have little to no effect on migratory birds.

The other objective of the AMPS group was to build support for the interstate. The AMPS director, J. L. Wade, was a master at promotion. Mr. Wade, Mary Lee Clostermery, and Tom Coulson came up with the slogan "Bridge the Gap." The AMPS board liked it and used it in all of our public relations materials.

AMPS had a number of promotional activities. Two really successful activities were when the Quincy Jaycees walked on the route of the proposed highway to Springfield and swam across the Illinois River, where the bridges were to be built. Twenty-five to thirty Jaycees swam across the river. The event received a lot of press coverage with media from Quincy to Springfield. My daughter, Lisa, was sixteen years old at the time and had just passed her lifeguard test. Bill Tate, AMPS director and owner of Tate Cheese, and I told Lisa she should swim with the Jaycees in case they needed help. All of the swimmers made it across, and it was a great experience for Lisa. The other activity we had was an open house attended by nearly twenty-five hundred people for the two new half-completed bridges over the Illinois River. The bridges were named the Valley City Eagle Bridges and were dedicated on Saturday, October 13, 1990.

These and other activities kept the public's attention on the highway all five years of the construction process. The delay in the construction was caused by the Illinois and US Highway Departments making two poor decisions. One was not completing the 4(f) document, and the other was using bridge replacement funds and leaving the old bridge for Route 36. The AMPS board could have publicly been very critical of both the state and federal agencies, but we knew that they were the same people that would make the decisions on when and where the highway would be built. So, although privately we did not agree with how it was handled, we understood that in order to meet our objective of completing the project, it was better not to criticize.

After working through the courts and getting the legislation passed for the funding, we thought our task was going to get easier, but we were about to have another problem. A group of local citizens had visited with Governor Thompson and other political leaders in Springfield and asked for a rest area and visitor center to be built along the interstate near New Philadelphia in Pike County. New Philadelphia, Illinois, was the first town in America plotted and registered by a freed slave, Free Frank McWhorter. We met with Governor Thomson about this issue. He said the rest area would cost more than $1 million to build and delay the highway at least another year. He also said it was a valuable site and deserved recognition.

There was no way that people in West Central Illinois and Northeast Missouri were going to support delaying the highway another year. A longtime doctor from Griggsville had recently been killed driving on old Route 104 going to Jacksonville. The two highways, US 36 and IL 104, were old, narrow, and dangerous roads. They were not built to handle the amount of traffic traveling on them across West Central Illinois from Quincy to Springfield. People wanted the four-lane highway now.

The AMPS board decided to go to the press. I made this statement: "We will support and work to get New Philadelphia preserved and recognized as an important part of our history, but we will not do anything that will delay this highway for one day or add one dollar to the cost."

It took ten years to complete the highway from the bridges over the Illinois River to the bridge over the Mississippi River at Hannibal, Missouri. The bridge over the Mississippi River was opened September 16, 2000, signifying the end of the project. I attended the bridge dedication ceremony along with many governmental officials

After the ceremony was over, I told Missouri Governor Mel Carnahan and Illinois Lieutenant Governor Bob Kustra about our pledge to promote New Philadelphia. They both agreed to help. However, shortly after that Governor Carnahan was killed in a plane crash, and Lieutenant Governor Kustra resigned and took the job as president of the University of Eastern Kentucky.

I was committed to following through with our pledge to support New Philadelphia. AMPS directors Harry Wright, Joe Conover, and myself as president of AMPS got a group together and formed an Illinois not for profit 501c (3) corporation named New Philadelphia Association (NPA) to promote the town of New Philadelphia.

The first activity of NPA was to mark the New Philadelphia town site with a nice, well-built sign to replace the small wooden sign that had been put up many years before by the Pike County Historical Association. NPA started looking for a university or an organization to work with to research the site. We knew that we would need more detailed information about the historical significance of this town and the founding father, Free Frank McWhorter. As we talked to various people about the work and research that needed to be done, the University of Maryland kept coming up along with Dr. Paul Shackel's name. The Illinois State Museum and Dr. Terry Martin, PhD, also expressed interest.

The University of Illinois at Springfield had just hired Dr. Vibert White, PhD, to teach African American History. Dr. Richard Ringeisen was appointed chancellor at the University of Illinois in Springfield and gave Dr. White a grant to hold a seminar on New Philadelphia. This brought some of the right people together to start making plans on how we should move forward.

Dr. Shackel received a grant to do archaeological work at the site. He and Dr. Martin conducted an archaeological training school at the site for three years. Dr. Chris Fennell with the University of Illinois at Champaign and Dr. Martin received another grant and did three more years of field study.

The research results helped lay the groundwork for all the future efforts. In 2005 the town site was named to the National Register of Historic Places. Also, that year, Illinois designated I-72 between Griggsville and Hull the Free Frank McWhorter Memorial Highway. The town site was designated as a National Historic Landmark in 2009 and in 2013 was included in the National Park Service's National Underground Railroad Network to Freedom program. A walking trail was established at the site along with a kiosk to educate visitors about how Free Frank had established the town and helped to free other slaves.

In 2014 President Obama signed legislation to authorize the National Park Service to conduct a special resources study of New Philadelphia's qualifications to become a unit of the National Park Service. A virtual reality tour was added on the walking trail and additional story signs were placed in the kiosk. Then in 2017 the Smithsonian American History Museum opened its "Many Voices, One Nation" exhibit featuring the McWorter family and artifacts from the New Philadelphia site.

My first exposure to the Smithsonian was through Congressman Paul Findley. The Smithsonian had constructed an exhibit about the Enola Gay, the plane that carried the atomic bomb dropped on Japan on August 6, 1945. Paul Tibbets, the pilot of the Enola Gay, was from Quincy, Illinois. Veteran groups called for the Smithsonian to put the Enola Gay on display in the early 1980s. This led to a bitter debate over historical context. Congressman Findley was a World War II veteran and was involved in this debate.

I had the opportunity to visit the Smithsonian in the early 2000s with some of my grandchildren. I was surprised to find no exhibits focused on agriculture and farming. It didn't seem right for one of our country's most important industries to be missing in one of the country's most prestigious museums. I decided to do something about it.

Sharon Covert was serving with me on USB. She was the past chairwoman of the Illinois Soybean Checkoff Board and had experience at helping museums develop agricultural exhibits. Sharon had connections with people associated with the Smithsonian. As chairman of USB, I asked Sharon to research how we could get more agriculture related exhibits in the Smithsonian. After many years of hard work, the new American Enterprise exhibit opened at the Smithsonian. Thanks to Sharon the new exhibit has numerous agricultural displays.

Working on the ag exhibit provided me a chance to meet and connect with many folks from the Smithsonian. I used this opportunity to mention New Philadelphia and lay the groundwork for establishing an exhibit that would tell the story of Frank McWhorter. The Smithsonian staff was very interested in the idea and eventually approved the exhibit on the McWhorter family and New Philadelphia.

The next step is for the New Philadelphia town site to become a unit of the National Park System. It will once again require the House and Senate to pass legislation and for the president to sign it. Something tells me that I will likely be involved in that. It's proof that a road in the middle of nowhere can definitely lead you somewhere unexpected, such as from Griggsville to the Smithsonian!

19

A Walk from Kentucky

The many journeys that I have embarked on in my lifetime have led me around the world, but none compare to the journey that my grandfather, Samuel (Sam) Sanders Bradshaw, took when he walked from Kentucky to Illinois.

Sam was born in Green County, Kentucky, on April 25, 1871. He was one of ten children born to Abraham and Florilla Noe Bradshaw. At the age of seventeen, Sam left Kentucky and walked to Indianapolis, Indiana. This was more than a two-hundred-mile trek. He found work doing whatever he could to earn money. Then in 1889 he decided to travel to Springfield, Illinois, to see Abraham Lincoln's hometown. He walked west until he eventually reached Springfield.

While doing odd jobs in Springfield, Sam heard of the good jobs being offered in Pike County due to the rapidly expanding railroads crossing the area. He decided to head farther west in hopes of better opportunities. He could have taken the train to Pike County, but the tickets cost too much. Having walked from Kentucky to Indiana and then Indiana to Springfield, the seventy-plus-mile walk from Springfield to Pike County probably seemed like a walk in the park.

Upon arriving in Pike County, Sam got his first job hewing railroad ties for a railroad company south of Perry, Illinois. Soon after getting his first job, he purchased a sawmill and started sawing lumber and railroad ties. This proved to be a very good business, but it took three of his fingers and left his other arm severely deformed from a bad bone break.

Sam was not only successful in starting a new business in Pike County but also in finding his true love. He met Lurena (Rena) Ann Manton from the Perry area. They were married and had twelve children between 1898 and 1920.

Phil's grandparents, Sam and Lurena Bradshaw (Photo courtesy of Phil Bradshaw.)

My grandfather was a big believer in education even though he had only been able to attend school until the sixth grade. He moved his family to where my cousin lives now, just one mile west of Griggsville. Grandpa purchased this big house and farm near town so his children could all attend the local high school. He built a sidewalk from their home to where the city sidewalk ended so his large family of children could walk to school. He had to make two little bridges across the creek. That was the extent that grandpa went to ensure that all twelve of his children received an education. My father and his brothers and sisters walked to school every day, walked home for lunch, and walked back to school in the afternoon. I do not know if all of my aunts and uncles went on beyond high school, but I do know Aunt Alice and Aunt Rachel went to my alma mater, Western Illinois University, for two years and became schoolteachers.

Grandpa Sam continued to run the sawmill and added a threshing machine business. Along with his sons, Clyde, Tom (my father), and Walter, he threshed grain for farmers all around Pike County.

The Bradshaw brothers, left to right*: Walter, Tom, Arthur, Clyde, George, and Roscoe in 1970. (Photo courtesy of Phil Bradshaw.)*

Grandpa's threshing machine would run with a long belt from a steam engine. My uncle Clyde would pull the threshing machine from farm to farm to thresh wheat and oats. The wheat and oats were cut with a binder and then put in bundles, which were stacked in the field. The bundles were then hauled to the threshing machine, where the grain was threshed, and the straw was piled in the big straw pile. It took three or four wagons pulled by teams of horses to haul the bundles from the field to the threshing machine and then took one or two more teams of horses to haul the grain away.

My grandfather was a very ambitious young man. He was farming with his in-laws, the Mantons, and renting some other land, raising cattle on most of it. Through his hard work and shrewd business sense, he accumulated over two thousand acres of farmland and timber, along with the local grain elevator, the fairgrounds, a filling station, four houses, and the bank in Griggsville, which closed in 1931. He purchased a small amount of stock in the new bank in Griggsville when it opened in 1942.

This list of assets came with a hefty price tag. The Bradshaw farm was heavily indebted, owing over $250,000 in 1932 when my father graduated from high school. This would be the equivalent of more than $4 million in today's money. My father, Tom, dedicated most of his life to paying off the debt my grandfather had accumulated.

On April 13, 1939, the day that I was born, Adolf Hitler was preparing to invade Poland, which would lead to the beginning of World War II. During this time the United States was starting to recover from the worst economic depression the country had ever seen. Most farmers were struggling to keep their farms afloat after six or seven years of severely depressed prices.

Tom Bradshaw and his wife, Lois, lived in Griggsville in a small rented house across the street from the junior high and high school. They had a three-year-old son, Frederick Lee, and were expecting the birth of their second child at any moment. Rather than taking his pregnant wife to the hospital in the old truck that delivered coal to homes around the Griggsville community, Tom borrowed his older brother's car for the fifty-mile trip to the hospital in Quincy, where I was born.

Dad and Mother did not know what to expect from this new little baby. My brother, Fred, had provided them some stressful times, such as when he escaped on his tricycle and went almost a mile west of town. As a three-year-old, he had decided that he was going to grandpa's house, and to his credit he made it there but got into big trouble.

As a young boy, I spent as much time as I could helping my dad, uncles, and grandpa on the farm. It's not like I really had a choice in the matter. Back in those days farming was very labor intensive. There was always plenty of work to do, and if you were an able body, you were given a job to do. It was hard work, but I also enjoyed being outside and working with my family.

Grandpa had almost four hundred cows, a few chickens, a few pigs, and several horses. With that many cows to feed, we were constantly baling hay. You may have heard the expression "Make hay while the sun shines." Well, I lived that expression. We baled alfalfa, clover, and grass hay every day the weather was fit from the time I was born until I was out of college. At that time, Dad purchased a Hesston hay stacker, and most farmers were starting to use big round bales handled by tractor and loader. I purchased a big round baler after I started farming.

Up until the mid-1940s most of the hay used to feed the livestock was stored loose in barns. The hay would be cut with a small mower pulled by horses. Knives moved back and forth as the wheels of the mower turned. The hay was then allowed to dry in the sun and would be picked up with a buck rake that made small piles of hay in the field. Then men would use pitchforks to pick up the hay and load it onto wagons, which were then hauled to the barn. A horse would pull hay up into the barn with a grapple hook, and a trip rope would drop the hay where you wanted it in the barn. The rope would be fastened to the barn about six or seven feet out from the gable of the barn. A pulley would then let the rope go to the other end of the barn and back down to the horse. Many times, this horse, called the hay horse, would be ridden by a younger child, since all the horse was doing was going back and forth. I was too young to ever ride the hay horse, but I can remember my brother, Fred, riding the hay horse at my uncle Charlie Myers's farm.

Uncle Charlie and Aunt Veda were more like grandparents to me than my aunt and uncle. Aunt Veda was twelve years older than my mother. At age twelve my mother had gone to live with her sister and her husband, because they lived in the Griggsville school district, and this allowed mother to attend high school. My mother's parents lived on a little farm east of Perry, and Grandmother Sweeting continued to live there even after her husband passed away.

The process for producing hay changed greatly as balers came on the market. The early balers were stationary, so you had to bring the hay to the baler. The first baler that I remember required two people to ride on the side of the baler. One individual poked the wires through the hay and the other individual, on the other side of the bale, tied the wire. If you wanted a dirty job that was it. The plunger from the baler would hit the hay every time it pushed it together and shoved all the dust and dirt right in your face. Then my grandfather purchased a Minneapolis Moline baler that made the heaviest bales I can ever remember. Unfortunately, it only worked about half the time, but it increased the amount of hay we could put in the barn because it automatically tied the bales. When that baler wore out, we purchased a New Holland baler. This new baler made smaller bales that weren't so heavy. This baler would bale a lot of hay.

The advancement of farm machinery helped farmers improve their production. As better and bigger tractors and equipment came onto the market, that also allowed them to farm more acres with less labor. Most of the farmers, including us, were slowly replacing the horses and mules with tractors. The number of acres of grass and oats required to feed horses was going down because we no longer needed to use horses to do the field work.

My grandfather first purchased an old steam engine to run a sawmill. Later he purchased an old steam tractor with all steel wheels. This was an oil-burning tractor that could actually move and do some of the things the horses did. Sometime in the 1930s Grandpa got his first gasoline-powered Case steel wheel tractors. They were quite an improvement to the old Rumely's steam tractor and steam engines.

Corn, which was our main crop, was harvested by hand until the early 1940s.

A farmer shucks corn by hand. (Photo courtesy of Library of Congress—Farm Security Administration—Office of War Information Photograph Collection.)[21]

I can remember my father, my uncles, and other laborers going to the cornfield with a team of horses and shucking corn by hand. A good day might be to harvest one hundred bushels by hand, and this would be a long day. Now I can sit in the climate-controlled cab of a combine and harvest fifteen hundred to two thousand bushels in *one* hour.

The combine is an amazing machine. It harvests the ear of corn from the plant, shells the corn from the cob, cleans the corn, and then dumps the corn into the storage tank of the combine. The stalks, leaves, shucks, and cobs are blown out the back of the combine onto the ground. This residue protects the soil from wind and water erosion and helps lower the weed population, therefore using less herbicide.

One combine can harvest multiple crops such as soybeans, wheat, oats, and rice by using different heads. A farmer can change from a forty-two-foot soybean head to a thirty-six-row corn head in thirty minutes. This makes it possible to harvest corn in the morning and soybeans in the afternoon.

The combine has a computer monitor connected to a GPS system that instantly tracks and records several pieces of information while the crop is being harvested, such as the moisture of the grain and the yield per acre. The combine, while doing all of these things, can also be steered automatically by using GPS technology.

All of this information can be overlaid with other pieces of information collected throughout the growing season such as the hybrid seed planted and number of seeds planted per acre, soil fertility levels, and herbicides and fungicides applied. Nowadays, farmers are not only harvesting crops, we are also harvesting data to make more informed decisions that benefit both the farmer and the environment.

A combine is usually one of the most expensive pieces of equipment that a farmer owns, costing from $300,000 to $700,000 according to the size of the machine and how it is equipped. While it is expensive, I wouldn't want to go back to picking corn by hand!

A modern Case IH combine harvests corn with an eight-row cornhead. (Photo courtesy of Justin Waack, Waack Creative.)

Soon after World War II, Grandpa purchased a Massey Harris self-propelled two-row corn picker. A Massey Harris implement business had opened in Griggsville, and this was the only implement business I ever knew in Griggsville. We purchased mostly Massey Harris tractors since there was a dealership close by. Grandpa had by this time purchased two 101 Massey Harris tractors with rubber tires and had also purchased two 22 Massey Harris tractors. The 101's were about thirty-five horsepower and the 22's were about twenty horsepower. He later purchased two 44 Massey Harris tractors, which were around forty-five horsepower and would pull a three-bottom sixteen-inch moldboard plow. The 22 tractors were used to mow and rake hay and cultivate corn. The 22 was one of the first tractors I ever drove. The first tractor that you got to drive by yourself was always a memorable moment for a farm boy. This was a rite of passage and one step toward becoming a man.

I still use Massey tractors on our farm. My brothers, Harvey and Freddie, switched to using John Deere tractors on their farms in the early to mid-1960s, but I stayed with Massey.

Phil with his brothers, Fred, on the left, *and Harvey,* on the right. *(Photo courtesy of Phil Bradshaw.)*

Similar to purchasing a certain brand of car, there are pros and cons about certain brands of tractors. John Deere tractors were built in Illinois and had better dealerships, but they were a little more expensive than the Masseys. I've always felt like the Massey tractors are a part of my family's farming heritage.

Uncle Clyde purchased a self-propelled combine in the 1950s. It was a very modern and very nice machine. This created a tremendous change with no more shocking of the wheat or oats. The combine did all the work of harvesting the grain all in one pass. We also purchased an elevator that would move the corn from the wagons up into the corn cribs so you no longer had to scoop the corn by hand.

As I look back over my years on the farm, one of the biggest changes that I have seen is the improvement in the farm machinery and equipment. The early tractors had small horsepower, no cab, no automatic transmission, no radio, and very little spring in the seat. Compare this to today's tractors with cabs, automatic transmissions, Global Positioning System (GPS), auto steer, monitors for all kinds of things and some with four-hundred-plus horsepower. The cab on tractors and combines was one of the biggest improvements for farmers. The cab made tractors and combines safer; you had protection from falling off and from turning over the tractor or combine. In addition, the cabs helped keep farmers out of the weather and out of the dust.

Monitors on corn planters were another big improvement made over the years. I can remember planting twenty acres of corn with a four-row planter. This took most of the day, and after I finished planting the field I realized that one row was not working and had not planted any corn. I had to go back and plant the one row again, which took just as long the second time. Today, planters can plant up to forty-eight rows and plant hundreds of acres a day. They have GPS with auto steer, which keeps the rows evenly spaced while following the contour of a field. The planter monitor constantly tells you how many seeds are being planted in each row, the total population of seeds planted per acre, and how deep the seed is planted. The planter using GPS can shut off any rows that come into contact with ground that has already been planted. This saves on the amount of seed that is used and from overplanting the end rows.

Hybrid seed corn was introduced in the 1930s. Up until that time open pollinated corn had been planted. This basically was seed from the corn raised the year before. Hybrid seed corn was produced by inbreeding the best traits from one corn family line to another corn family line, producing the best qualities of both in the hybrid seed.

Commercial seed corn companies were able to produce large quantities of hybrid seed in a short amount of time. This was beneficial to farmers as it would have taken years for a farmer to raise enough hybrid seed for his own use. Yields in the 1940s increased for many reasons, but hybrid seed corn producing higher yields and stronger plants was one of the more significant reasons. This was the first successful time that man was able to control genes in corn to increase yield. Seventy-some years later genetically modified plants are common, thanks to improved technology.

During my lifetime things changed dramatically in the livestock industry. In the 1940s most people had ten to twelve sows that would have piglets twice a year. During the wintertime the sows would be shut up in small sheds or any place that they could keep warm. We would use straw that had been baled from wheat fields during the summer for their bedding in the winter. Four or five pigs weaned per litter were the average per sow. Now that number is ten to eleven pigs weaned per sow.

The cattle business changed as well. More cattle were being fed to market weight on grain, mostly corn and some supplement, instead of a diet mainly on grass or hay. The corn-based rations allowed the cattle to gain weight faster and provided a better steak with more marbling. Most farmers in the Midwest would either raise or purchase calves to place in feedlots, typically less than one hundred head. Calves would be weaned from the mother cows at around four hundred pounds or purchased and brought in from the West or Southwest. Farmers would usually begin feeding calves in the fall and would feed the calf approximately one pound for every hundred pounds the calf weighed, plus all the hay they could eat. In the spring the calves would be put out on grass.

In midsummer to early fall, farmers would start to feed their previous year's calves, called yearlings. Yearling calves that weighed about six hundred pounds each were fed on about one pound of corn per one hundred pounds of weight. We would gradually increase the amount of corn we fed them, and in two or three weeks they would be up to full feed, where they would eat two to two and a half pounds of corn per one hundred pounds of weight. We would then feed them until they weighed twelve hundred pounds and were ready for market. Most cattle were hauled by train or truck to a terminal market near large cities where meat was needed. For their own family's use, farmers processed their own cattle and hogs either at home or at a custom slaughtering plant. This provided meat year-round.

Before we had a refrigerator, we used an icebox to store our food. In the winter, Grandpa would go to the Illinois River four miles east of

Griggsville and cut out blocks of ice. He would bring them home and put them in the ice house and cover the ice with sawdust from the sawmill so we would have ice for the iceboxes all summer.

Gardening was a necessity back in those days as the produce helped feed our families, but it provided a time for fellowship and made many family memories also. Dad and Mother had a small garden at home, but there were also two big gardens for the entire family. One was at an old abandoned house, which was one quarter of a mile east of where we lived and about one fourth of a mile from Grandpa and Uncle Walter. We would all get together to plant the garden after Dad, Uncle Walter, or Grandpa had plowed it up. It was more than a half an acre, which was originally the front yard of the house. I always figured it was better to have a bigger garden than a bigger yard. I would help cut the eyes out of the potatoes and plant them in the little furrow that had been made across the length of the garden. There was also a large garden at Grandpa's house where we planted tomatoes, cucumbers, green beans, peas, carrots, cabbage, lettuce, radishes, turnips, sweet potatoes, and other products.

I can still remember how good the vegetables tasted right out of the garden. Grandpa was the one who got me to like raw cucumbers. He would pick cucumbers off the vine in the garden and give me one to eat. We would clean them by wiping them off on our dirty jeans and then just eat them right down. There were apple, peach, and pear trees around the different family members' homes and blackberries in the timber around the fields. We truly relied on the land for our family's food with various vegetables and fruits harvested throughout the year. There were catfish in the creek and of course beef, pork, and chicken from the farm. It all made for good eating!

Many people refer to these days as "the good ol' days." When I think of all the hard work and physical labor, I don't think of them as particularly good. The thing that made these days good was working closely with your family.

20 My Journey to Feed the World

As I look back on the seventy-five-plus years of my life and my travels, I realize that all of my journeys have led me down the same path—to help feed the world. My entire life has revolved around food and ultimately taking care of people either by being active in ag groups and having the opportunity to travel around the world or by actually producing crops and livestock on my farm.

The objective of most of the trips that I took on behalf of the various ag groups was focused on improving food production in one way or another. Whether in Bolivia helping to stamp out foot and mouth disease or in Romania helping farmers use soybean meal in their livestock feed, improving food production was the main objective for my journeys.

In addition, the journey that I embarked on as a farmer and all the many changes that I have experienced on the farm were slowly moving to better farming practices that increased production. In the end, my life's journey has paralleled agriculture's journey of increasing food production for a growing population.

Food—it's a basic need for our existence. We need food to survive and thrive. From the beginning of time man has sought food to feed his family—from gathering berries and nuts, to hunting game to learning how to cultivate crops and domesticate livestock. The journey has been long and continues still today. What we eat and how that food is produced has changed over time. This journey of food production has not only increased the amount of food that we have to eat, but we have improved the way we raise our food and the quality of our food.

Food is one of those things that you take for granted until your stomach begins to rumble, and then it becomes a priority. Let me stress that I realize that hunger is a very real problem in our country and around the world. Unfortunately, I have seen firsthand malnourished, starving children and the look of pain and despair in their eyes. While we may have enough food available as a society that doesn't mean that it ends up in the mouths of people who need it. According to Feeding America, the leading hunger organization in the United States, forty-one million people struggled in 2016 with hunger in the United States, including thirteen million children.[22] Worldwide some 795 million people do not have enough food to lead a healthy, active life, which is about one in nine people on earth.[23] Hunger is caused not only by production challenges that impact the amount of food available, but also by the challenges of distributing the food that is produced. Political, economic, and social issues in some cases keep people from having the food they need.

Farmers have done such a good job at what they do—raising crops, vegetables, fruits, and livestock—that the majority of the US population has been able to remove the worry about having enough food from their minds. A consistent and nutritious food supply has helped our country develop into the world power that we are.

Today, we as consumers have an enormous amount of food choices. According to the Food Marketing Institute, between 1975 and 2008, the number of products in the average supermarket exploded from an average of 8,948 to almost 47,000.[24] I don't usually do the grocery shopping and can probably count on one hand the number of times that I have gone to the grocery store by myself. I do enjoy going to the grocery store with Linda, but I don't think she enjoys my company. I'm like a little kid in a candy store, looking at all the new products that are in the aisles and within my reach. It's great that consumers have so many choices when it comes to food. This is possible because of the innovations and new technologies being used today.

While more choices overall are a good thing, it has led to more scrutiny by consumers about where their food comes from and how it is produced. At the same time, people are further removed from the farm. Years ago, many people had someone in their family—a grandparent or uncle or cousin—who farmed. They had a connection or a link to the land. As farmers grew more efficient, they were able to produce more food on fewer acres with fewer people. There became fewer and fewer farmers even as our population continued to grow. Many generations have lost that connection to where their food comes from. Today only 1 percent of our population is directly connected to production agriculture.

I think people have lost an appreciation for the people, the technology, the time, the dedication, the investment, and the blood, sweat, and tears that go into producing a pork chop or a bowl of corn flakes.

As production agriculture has changed from the early days of my farming career to where we are now, it has provided an opportunity for some to question if the changes have been beneficial, and that has created debates in public sectors. While an open dialogue is healthy on any issue, the discussion must be based on facts and not simply on emotions. The number of negative stories in the media about today's agriculture has been increasing over the last few decades. A lot of the national press was telling the story of modern agriculture production from what they were hearing from small groups and individuals, many of whom had little scientific knowledge and little farm production knowledge. It took me, along with several other ag leaders, several years to convince national farm organizations that we had to take control of telling the story of modern agriculture production.

To help accomplish this, many national ag groups came together and started the US Farmers & Ranchers Alliance (USFRA). This was initiated when I was chairman of USB in 2010. Bob Stallman, president of the American Farm Bureau, was selected the first chairman, and I was selected vice chairman. One of the first things the USFRA did was hire a firm to help determine a baseline of consumers' current views and thoughts on modern farming practices. We needed to know what people knew about these issues, where they were getting their information, and what could be done to move people back into a position of support for agriculture production.

Using focus groups all across the country, USFRA found that it was more a lack of understanding than a true fear of GMOs and other new ag technology. I and other farm group leaders received some heat over spending the money to establish this baseline. Many of my fellow farmers wanted to see TV ads during the Super Bowl and in other prominent places touting the benefits of American farmers and agriculture. However, those ads would have quickly depleted all of our money. The baseline focus groups showed an advertising campaign would not improve consumers' support of American farmers and agriculture by a noticeable amount. Rather, consumers wanted a dialogue to ask questions directly to farmers and to hear the pros and cons on various food-related issues.

Today USFRA consists of more than one hundred farmer- and rancher-led organizations and agricultural partners representing virtually all aspects of agriculture. USFRA works across the country to engage in dialogue with consumers who have questions about how today's food is grown and raised. They have held a number of activities and events with consumers, and the reports I have seen show the number of negative articles about agriculture have gone down. Those in production agriculture must be committed to continuous improvement in all that we do and support efforts to increase confidence and trust in today's agriculture.

In the 1990s, I heard Kofi Annan, UN secretary general, speak of the importance and influence business and industry had around the world, which in many cases affected people's lives more than governments do. In 1999, the UN Global Compact was launched by the United Nations to encourage businesses worldwide to adopt a sustainable-principle-based framework for businesses. It stated ten principles in areas of human rights, labor, the environment, and anticorruption. In 2010 when I was chairman of USB, I attended three or four UN Global Compact meetings. I decided not to continue attending because I thought it was becoming too political, and it might appear that I was lobbying, which I was not allowed to do as chairman. Although I was unable to attend the meetings, I felt it was a mistake for agriculture not to be represented at the UN Global Compact.

At one meeting there were approximately five hundred to one thousand people representing businesses and organizations from around the world. Only two of us at the meeting were actual farmers. The other registered farmer and his wife were from Argentina. He had flown to New York in his private jet and was there to meet with people who worked for him in New York. He was not a fair representation of the majority of farmers that I know. However, at some of the other meetings I attended, the United Nations had brought in peasant farmers from around the world to represent agriculture.

As far as I know, at this time there are no production ag groups involved in the Global Compact meetings. I would estimate that a majority of the discussions at these meetings is about food and agriculture related issues. I know most of my fellow farmers are not big supporters of the United Nations because it is believed to be very liberal and socialistic. However, I have always believed that we in production agriculture should be at the table to tell our own story.

Global population has been on the rise for the last one hundred years, and the trends don't show that this will be slowing down any time in the near future. Experts predict that by 2050 the world population could reach more than 9.7 billion people.[25] That's up from the most recent estimate of 7.3 billion people in the world today.[26] The increase in population along with the increase of incomes of developing countries, causing more people to want more meat and protein in their diets, will cause an increase in global food demand.

As we look toward the future, I believe that there will be more people taking more land out of production. That means more food will be needed to feed a growing population with less land available to produce food. In order to maintain an abundant, affordable, consistent, safe, nutritious food supply for people in the United States and around the world, we need more research in agriculture and food production. We must continually look for new ways of producing food, as well as transporting and preserving the food we produce. Farmers through their checkoff programs will continue to spend more money and time on research and new distribution systems for the food they produce. Farmers will need the help of everyone to keep food on the table for people around the world. Governments, consumer groups, nongovernment organizations, corporations and individuals, will all have to get more involved to ensure the food is there when it is needed.

My family has always been there for me, and I would not be where I am today without their help and support. The foundation that my parents, aunts, uncles, and grandparents prepared for me provided the opportunity for me to be successful. I have strived to provide the same support and foundation to my children and grandchildren for their success in the future. Now that my children and grandchildren are farming, it's exciting to think about what the future holds for agriculture. I think of the changes that I have seen in my life and anticipate that they will see even more drastic changes in how we raise food for a growing population.

Family and farming go hand in hand at Bradshaw Farms. Three generations of Bradshaws inspect the soybean crop—Phil (center)*, Todd Bradshaw, Phil's son* (left) *and Brock Willard, Phil's grandson* (right)*. (Photo provided by the United Soybean Board.)*

None of my journeys would have happened if my grandfather had not taken that courageous step to begin a journey that would directly shape my family and indirectly shape farming and agriculture. The journey is far from complete. I hope my story will inspire others to continue to get involved and help make a difference to continue down the path to help feed the world. God bless.

Phil and Linda with their children, grandchildren, and great-grandchildren in 2017 in front of their farm. Front Row: (l to r) Jonah Bradshaw, Todd Bradshaw, Ben Bradshaw, Carrie Bradshaw, Luke Bradshaw, Christy Willard Dempsey, Cindy Bradshaw Willard, Linda Bradshaw, Philip Bradshaw, Lisa Bradshaw, Jude Smith, Kasey Smith, Kason Sutton (Kasey's son) Back Row: (l to r) Brock Willard, Darrell Dempsey, Richard Willard, Mike White (Lisa), Tommy Craft (Rashelle), Josh Smith Not pictured Rashelle Pruett (Lisa's daughter) and Ayla Donovan (Rashelle's daughter) (Photo courtesy of Phil Bradshaw.)

Acronyms and Abbreviations

AMPS	Adams, Morgan, Pike and Scott Counties Interstate Highway Association
AMS	Agricultural Marketing Service
APHIS	Animal and Plant Health Inspection Service
ASA	American Soybean Association
BIFAD	Board for International Food & Agriculture Development
CGB	Consolidated Grain & Barge
CIA	Central Intelligence Agency
CIE	Central Illinois Expressway
EPA	Environmental Protection Agency
ERS	Economic Research Service
EU	European Union
FDIC	Federal Deposit Insurance Corporation
FMD	Foot-and-Mouth Disease
GATT	General Agreement on Tariffs and Trade
GIEFA	Inter-American Group for the Eradication of Foot-and-Mouth Disease
GMOs	genetically modified organisms
GPS	Global Positioning System
Hp	horsepower
IDOA	Illinois Department of Agriculture
IDOT	Illinois Department of Transportation
IFDC	International Fertilizer Development Center
IPPA	Illinois Pork Producers Association
LCI	Livestock Conservation Institute
NAFTA	North American Free Trade Agreement
NATO	North Atlantic Treaty Organization

NCBA	National Cattlemen's Beef Association
NPA	New Philadelphia Association
NPB	National Pork Board
NPPC	National Pork Producers Council
OCC	Office of Controller of Currency
OIE	Office of International Epizootics
OIG	Office of Inspector General
PAHO	Pan-American Health Organization
PANAFTOSA	Pan American Foot-and-Mouth Disease Center
PRV	pseudorabies
UK	United Kingdom
UN	United Nations
USAHA	United States Animal Health Association
USAID	United States Agency for International Development
USB	United Soybean Board
USDA	United States Department of Agriculture
USFRA	United States Farmers & Ranchers Alliance
USMEF	United States Meat Export Federation
USSEC	United States Soybean Export Council
VOCA	Volunteers in Overseas Cooperative Assistance
WISHH	World Initiative for Soy in Human Health
WIU	Western Illinois University

About the Author

Philip E. Bradshaw is first and foremost a farmer and has been for more than fifty-five years. He has experienced numerous agricultural changes, from farming with horses to using machinery with satellite guidance systems. He has a long history of involvement in agricultural organizations and activities that span the United States and around the world. His passion for involvement is all about trying to make people's lives better.

His list of credentials is lengthy and includes serving as president of three major state and three national agricultural organizations, as well as serving on advisory committees for six US secretaries of agriculture. Bradshaw has been a leader on the international level on animal health and soybean issues.

Phil and his wife, Linda, have three children, seven grandchildren, and four great-grandchildren and live on their farm near Griggsville in Pike County, Illinois.

About the Ghostwriter

Tim Maiers has always enjoyed writing, although this is his first experience in ghostwriting a book. In 2015, Tim and his wife, LeAnn, started Maiers Ag Consulting to utilize the twenty-plus years of experience in communications and public relations for local, state, and national commodity groups and other organizations. They have worked on a variety of projects advocating for agriculture and telling the stories of farmers.

As a third-generation farmer, Tim raises corn, soybeans and hay on his family farm and has a 100-head cow-calf operation and contract finishes pigs near Payson, IL in Adams County. Tim and LeAnn have three children.

Endnotes

1 Office of the United States Trade Representative, "U.S.-Mexico Trade Facts," https://ustr.gov/countries-regions/americas/mexico (July 8, 2018).

2 USDA, "Food expenditures by families and individuals as a share of disposable personal income," https://www.ers.usda.gov/webdocs/DataFiles/50606/FoodExpenditures_table7.xls?v=42395 (Aug. 1, 2016).

3 Vachon, J., photographer. (1940) Adjusting wire in stake. Corn planting, Jasper County, Iowa. Iowa Jasper County Jasper County. United States, 1940. May. [Photograph] Retrieved from the Library of Congress, https://www.loc.gov/item/2017719866/.

4 USDA, "Office of Communications, Timeline, Cholera," https://www.ars.usda.gov/oc/timeline/cholera/ (Dec. 18, 2016).

5 USDA, "APHIS FMD Factsheet," https://www.aphis.usda.gov/publications/animal_health/2013/fs_fmd_general.pdf (Aug. 7, 2017).

6 Footandmouthdiseaseinfo.org, "Fact Sheet: Industry Economics," http://www.footandmouthdiseaseinfo.org/factsheetindustryeconomics.aspx (Aug. 7, 2017).

7 A. M. Countryman and A. Hagerman, 2017, "Retrospective Economic Analysis of Foot and Mouth Disease Eradication in the Latin American Beef Sector," *Agribusiness: An International Journal* 33, no. 3: 257–73.

8 Cristina Fernandez de Kirchner, president of Argentina, "Remarks and Presentations made during the Fifth Summit of the Americas," http://www.summit-americas.org/V_Summit/remarks_arg_sp.pdf (Aug. 17, 2017), Google Translate was used to translate from Spanish to English.

9 Daniel Ortega, president of Nicaragua, "Remarks and Presentations made during the Fifth Summit of the Americas," http://www.summit-americas.org/V_Summit/remarks_nic_sp.pdf (Aug. 17, 2017), Google Translate was used to translate from Spanish to English.

10 Barack Obama, president of the United States, "Remarks and Presentations made during the Fifth Summit of the Americas," http://www.summit-mericas.org/V_Summit/remarks_usa_en.pdf (Aug. 17, 2017).
11 United Soybean Board, "Independent study shows checkoff returns more than five dollars for every dollar farmers invest," https://unitedsoybean.org/article/checkoff-produces-big-roi (Aug. 22, 2017).
12 National Oceanic and Atmospheric Administration Fisheries, "2011 Top 10 Favorite Seafoods in the United States," https://www.fisheries.noaa.gov/2011-top-10-favorite-seafoods-united-states (Aug. 22, 2017).
13 USDA, "Industry Insight: Checkoff Programs Empower Business," https://www.usda.gov/media/blog/2011/09/21/industry-insight-checkoff-programs-empower-business (Aug. 22, 2017).
14 National Pork Board, "U.S. Pork Exports Set New Volume Records in 2017," https://www.pork.org/news/u-s-pork-exports-set-new-volume-records-2017/ (Aug. 10, 2018).
15 National Pork Producers Council, "NPPC Statement On Farmer Aid Package," http://nppc.org/nppc-statement-on-farmer-aid-package/ (Aug. 10, 2018).
16 United Soybean Board, "Biodiesel," http://unitedsoybean.org/media-center/issue-briefs/biodiesel/ (Aug. 24, 2017).
17 Phyllis K. Fong, inspector general, letter to the Honorable Charles E. Grassley, https://www.usda.gov/oig/webdocs/Soybean_ltr_Sen_Grassley.pdf (Sept. 6, 2017).
18 Transcript of telephone conversation between Secretary of State Kissinger and Secretary of Agriculture Earl Butz, Washington, Oct. 16, 1975, 12:03 pm., *Foreign Relations of the United States 1969 to 1976*, vol. 16, document 209.
19 Fed Prime Rate, "Prime Rate History," http://www.fedprimerate.com/wall_street_journal_prime_rate_history.htm (Jan. 5, 2018).
20 FDIC, "The Banking Crises of the 1980s and Early 1990s: Summary and Implications," https://www.fdic.gov/bank/historical/history/3_85.pdf (Jan. 5, 2018).
21 United States Resettlement Administration, Lee, R., photographer, (1936), farmer handpicking corn near Aledo, Mercer County, Illinois, United States, 1936. Nov. [Photograph] retrieved from the Library of Congress, https://www.loc.gov/item/2017735002/.
22 Feeding America, "Facts about poverty and hunger in America," http://www.feedingamerica.org/hunger-in-america/facts.html (Feb. 23, 2018).
23 World Food Programme, "10 Facts About Hunger," https://www.wfp.org/stories/10-facts-about-hunger (Feb. 23, 2018).
24 Consumer Reports, "What to Do When There Are Too Many Product Choices on the Store Shelves?" https://www.consumerreports.org/cro/

magazine/2014/03/too-many-product-choices-in-supermarkets/index.htm (Feb. 23, 2018).

25 Food and Agriculture Organization of the United Nations, "The Future of Food and Agriculture, Trends and Challenges," http://www.fao.org/3/a-i6583e.pdf (Feb. 23, 2018).

26 Maarten Elferink and Florian Schierhorn, "Global Demand for Food is Rising. Can We Meet It?" https://hbr.org/2016/04/global-demand-for-food-is-rising-can-we-meet-it (Feb. 23, 2018).

Printed in the United States
by Baker & Taylor Publisher Services

Printed in the United States
by Baker & Taylor Publisher Services